Deliciously Healthy
Pregnancy

Deliciously Healthy
Pregnancy

Nutrition and recipes for optimal health
from conception to parenthood

RHIANNON LAMBERT

Contents

Preface

After falling pregnant with my first child, it became apparent that there wasn't much information available from nutritionists such as myself to guide us new mums-to-be through pregnancy. Right from the get-go, dangerously, the internet becomes your best friend, but it's hard to find much lifestyle and nutritional advice beyond what food and drink to avoid and a warning to not put on too much weight.

Before I became pregnant, I recorded an episode on fertility for my podcast *Food For Thought* after hearing the stats on how long it can take to get pregnant; the fact that it's just as much a man's responsibility as a woman's; and that there really never is the perfect time to get pregnant. That was the defining moment when I decided to try for a baby. I recall Dr Zoe Williams, ITV's media doctor, saying there was no harm in getting pregnant before your wedding and that, in fact, having your baby with you on your wedding day was pretty special. As it turned out, I walked down the aisle eight weeks' pregnant and gave birth in the peak of a global pandemic, not quite the fairytale I had hoped for.

I became fascinated by the world of antenatal, pregnancy, and postnatal nutrition. I enrolled in a university course and immersed myself in this little-discussed area. Managing a difficult pregnancy, working full-time running my clinic, then experiencing a traumatic birth meant this wasn't a perfect time, but it taught me a lot of life lessons. My career as a nutritionist truly helped me navigate this period, from preconception, through the trimesters, to recovering after the birth and starting on my breastfeeding journey. I yearned for an evidence-based book like this and I couldn't find one. Now, pregnant with my second baby and in the midst of nausea, I hope I can help you understand the role of nutrition in your pregnancy. I hope you won't need to trawl through endless online searches looking for advice. Instead you will be able to turn to this book that's full of information rooted in evidence that you can trust, alongside delicious recipes, to help you make it through those amazing, yet challenging, times of pregnancy and new motherhood.

I want to offer women the truth about nutrition in pregnancy. We all know that we need to eat well to help our babies grow, but good intentions can be hard to keep. Nausea, acid reflux, pain, discomfort, and an ever-increasing or decreasing appetite can all mean that pregnancy is not an easy journey. You may find you can't face a variety of foods, or are too worn out to spend much time cooking. As a health professional, I don't wish to preach the perfect pregnancy diet. I hope to inspire you, but also be a comfort and guiding hand. In the first section of this book, I explore how the food you eat and your amazing body supports the growth of your baby. The second part of the book has a range of delicious recipes, ideal for pregnancy, with pages 68–69 offering suggestions on which recipes can help you to combat the trials and tribulations of a particular trimester. I also haven't forgotten that you will be experiencing one of the most scary, exhilarating, and momentous moments of your life – birthing your child. The benefits of good nutrition don't end at this moment, they continue to aid you through the fourth trimester, the 12 weeks after the birth, a time when you need to heal and feed yourself and your baby. Here, you can choose simple recipes that can be rustled up easily with your baby in a sling or while asleep in their crib. All that's left for me to say is a huge congratulations and enjoy the delicious read ahead.

R Lamberl

@rhitrition

7

Living well for pregnancy and life

The food we eat and how we live impacts our health throughout life. This section sets out some highly researched ways of eating known to support health and happiness, exploring the benefits of a Mediterranean and plant-based approach; looks at how your body changes as your baby grows in pregnancy; and offers tailored nutritional and lifestyle advice to nurture you and your baby.

A Mediterranean approach

The Mediterranean diet originates from the olive-growing areas of this region. A focus on local, in-season ingredients matched with an active, outdoors lifestyle, has seen this way of life widely regarded as one of the healthiest worldwide. Adopting the diet's principles, or those of the closely aligned plant-based (not to be confused with vegan) diet (see p.14), has benefits throughout life and helps optimize the health of you and your baby in pregnancy.

A common focus

The Mediterranean way of eating varies from region to region, incorporating traditions from different countries, but each region has some common core principles. Generally, the diet is high in vegetables, fruits, pulses and beans, nuts, cereals, grains, fish, and unsaturated fats such as olive oil, and is low in saturated fats. An emphasis on freshness means foods are high in antioxidants and other important nutritional components such as fibre. While it's important to eat in a way that suits your cultural background and lifestyle, incorporating some components of a Mediterranean diet into your own will enable you to enjoy its many benefits.

How the Mediterranean diet enhances health

Extensive, up-to-date research shows that the Mediterranean way of eating – and its lifestyle – has many important benefits for our health. At times when the quality of our nutritional intake is particularly key, such as during pregnancy, following this eating model is especially helpful.

- **It supports our heart health**. A range of evidence suggests that the Mediterranean diet can reduce the risk of developing cardiovascular disease. One landmark study showed that this way of eating lowered the incidence of serious cardiovascular incidents. This is likely to be thanks to the focus on wholegrain carbohydrates and eating fewer animal products, which in turn reduces "bad" cholesterol lipids, called low-density lipoproteins (LDLs), associated with cardiovascular disease. The diet is also rich in polyunsaturated and monounsaturated fatty acids and fibrous foods, all linked to improved heart health. Overall, eating a Mediterranean-style diet is associated with healthy weight management and lower blood pressure.

- **It may help protect against cancer**. Healthy fats, plenty of fibre and antioxidants, and fewer processed foods, may explain why this lifestyle is associated with a reduced risk of developing some cancers, including breast, colorectal, gastric, head and neck, and prostate cancers.

- **It may help reduce the risk of diabetes**. Following a Mediterranean diet has been linked to both the prevention of diabetes and an overall improvement in blood glucose control.

- **It may help to slow cognitive decline**. Though inconclusive, there is evidence that a Mediterranean diet may offer some protection against cognitive diseases such as Alzheimer's and Parkinson's and it has been linked to a slower rate of decline generally in memory and cognitive processes. Though it's unclear why this is, it's thought that the antioxidant-rich diet may help to reduce the damaging inflammation that is found in some cognitive diseases.

- **It can enhance health in pregnancy**. Overall, eating a Mediterranean-style diet in pregnancy, together with taking supplements including folic acid and vitamin D (see p.58), will help to keep you and your baby well nourished. This way of eating may also have specific pregnancy benefits. A recent UK trial involving mums-to-be from five maternity units found that following this type of diet (in the trial, the women specifically ate 30g/1oz of mixed nuts a day and used extra virgin olive oil) could help to avoid excess weight gain in pregnancy and, in turn, lower the risk of developing gestational diabetes – diabetes that develops for the first time in pregnancy. Evidence on the benefits of a Mediterranean diet has led the US to recommend it in their dietary guidelines for pregnant women. The links between this way of eating and a reduction in the risk of gestational diabetes, together with its heart healthy associations, make it probable that a Mediterranean-style diet is likely to be recommended increasingly in pregnancy.

Colourful, fresh produce and olive oil *are staples of the heart-healthy Mediterranean diet.*

Adopting a Mediterranean way of eating

While access to local and seasonal produce can vary from region to region, there is still plenty you can do to adopt a Mediterranean style of eating at home. Observing the eating habits of Mediterranean families highlights the emphasis placed on healthy fats that are rich in monounsaturated and polyunsaturated (or essential omega-3) fatty acids, found in olive oil and oily fish – two key staples of the diet. In the UK, our consumption of saturated fat (too high) and oily fish (too low) is less than ideal. In addition, upping your intake of fruit and vegetables is also beneficial, as is reducing your consumption of red and processed meats. Follow the suggestions below to help you incorporate the key elements of a Mediterranean diet into your daily routine. You don't need to achieve an ideal balance of foods with each meal (see p.41), but aim to work foods in over the course of a day or a week.

- **Base your meals on complex carbohydrates** (see p.48) including bread, potatoes, and pasta. While some white pasta and bread is fine (and may be easier to face in pregnancy) aim to build in wholegrains to increase your fibre intake. Avoid highly refined carbs, making snacks such as pastries and sugary processed foods an occasional part of your diet.
- **Eat plenty of fruit and vegetables**. Aim for at least five portions of a variety of fruit and vegetables each day.
- **Choose products** made from vegetable and plant oils, such as olive oil and rapeseed oil.
- **Include sources of protein**. Focus on beans and pulses, fish, eggs, poultry, and other proteins, and eat red meat just occasionally. Fish is a regular part of a Mediterranean diet – try to eat two portions a week, one of which should be oily.
- **Eat some dairy** or fortified dairy alternatives, such as soya drinks. Opting for low-fat dairy can help control your intake of saturated fat.
- **Choose unsaturated oils** and spreads such as olive oil, using small amounts only.
- **Drink six to eight glasses** of fluid a day, or in pregnancy, eight to 10 glasses a day (see p.42).
- **Limit foods and drinks** that are high in fat, salt, or sugar, consuming these less often and in small amounts.

A plant-based diet

Following a plant-based diet means focusing primarily on foods from plants. This is not the same as vegan or vegetarian diets, which exclude all meat and, for vegans, dairy. Like the Mediterranean diet (see pp.10–13), a plant-based diet helps you to limit your intake of saturated fats, supporting your heart and overall health.

Getting all the essential nutrients

If you opt for a plant-based diet, it is important to plan your meals carefully to get enough of the nutrients that are found in larger amounts in animal products. If you are pregnant or breastfeeding, eating mainly plant-based foods can make it challenging to meet your newly increased need for nutrients such as vitamin D, calcium, iodine, folic acid, iron, essential omega-3 fatty acids, and vitamin B12. Eating a wide variety of plant-based foods will help to maximize your nutrient intake and provide energy. Pages 48–56 explore the plant food sources for these nutrients, and supplements may also be needed (see p.58).

Eat plenty of complex carbs (see p.48) with a range of vegetables and fruits. For meals without meat, fish, dairy, or eggs, include the following:

- **Plant-based protein sources** (see opposite). Soya products, such as tofu, tempeh, and edamame beans, are good sources of plant-based protein. Beans, lentils, and pulses also provide protein as well as essential vitamins and minerals – try chickpeas, red lentils, black beans, peas, and peanuts. Baked beans count, too, but opt for varieties with reduced or no sugar. Bear in mind that some vegan milk alternatives such as almond or oat milk are not a source of protein.
- **Sources of plant-based calcium**. This mineral can be hard for the body to absorb, with calcium from some plant-based foods absorbed more readily than from others. The calcium in cruciferous vegetables such as kale, fortified plant milks, and calcium-set tofu is well absorbed

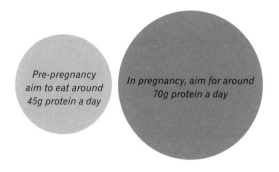

Pre-pregnancy aim to eat around 45g protein a day

In pregnancy, aim for around 70g protein a day

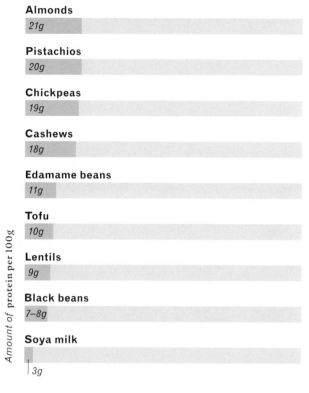

Almonds
21g

Pistachios
20g

Chickpeas
19g

Cashews
18g

Edamame beans
11g

Tofu
10g

Lentils
9g

Black beans
7–8g

Soya milk
3g

Amount of protein per 100g

Plant-based sources of protein

The protein requirements above will vary between individuals. The table, right, shows the amount of protein per 100g in some plant-based foods. It's important to eat a range of plant sources to get all the amino acids your body needs (see p.48)

(100g/3½oz of calcium-fortified tofu provides around half the recommended daily intake). Calcium from beans and pulses is fairly well absorbed, while calcium in sesame seeds and spinach is poorly absorbed.

- **Healthy plant-based fat sources**. A daily handful of nuts and seeds has a variety of healthy unsaturated fats. Omega-3 essential fatty acids (see p.51) in particular are key for heart health. Plant-based sources include walnuts, soya beans, chia seeds, flaxseeds, and rapeseed oil. The omega-3 in these foods is called alpha-lipoic acid (ALA), which converts in the body to eicosapentaenoic acid (EPA) and docosahexaenoic acid (DHA), found mostly in oily fish. If you don't eat these foods regularly, consider taking an algae-based omega-3 supplement (see p.59).

- **Other considerations**. Some nutrients, such as vitamins B2 and B12, can be scarce in a plant-based diet, so supplements and/or fortified foods (which can add vitamins, calcium, iron, iodine, and folic acid) can help. When you do eat animal-based foods, opt mainly for nutrient-dense eggs and dairy, choosing low-fat – and in pregnancy safe – cheeses (see pp.60–61).

Your pre-pregnancy diet

For some couples, becoming pregnant is relatively straightforward, while others find it takes a bit of time. For all couples, optimizing nutrition while trying to conceive helps to ensure the best possible nutritional start to pregnancy. Studies have also looked at the possible role of nutrition in fertility, and while there are no conclusive findings, data suggests that certain lifestyles and ways of eating are likely to favour more positive fertility outcomes.

The basics

Understanding the menstrual cycle and your "fertility window" – the few days before and the day after ovulation, which usually occurs around days 11 to 14 in an average 28-day cycle, when you are at your most fertile – is the first step in trying to conceive. Out of every 100 couples trying for a baby, 80 to 90 become pregnant within one year. The remaining couples will need more time, and some of them may need to turn to fertility treatments such as in vitro fertilization (IVF) to help them conceive.

Why nutrition and lifestyle count

While many factors contribute to conception, your diet and lifestyle can play an important role. Lifestyle factors such as stress, lack of sleep, and smoking can negatively impact fertility, as can obesity or extreme weight loss, poor digestion, and medical factors such as low immunity. What you eat and drink may also improve or hamper your fertility, with a healthy diet thought to help optimize egg and sperm health and the chances of conception, and possibly reduce the time it takes to conceive. It's thought that reducing caffeine and alcohol intake may lower the risk of miscarriage, although in most cases miscarriage is due to issues beyond an individual's control such as genetic, anatomical, or hormonal factors.

A fertility and pregnancy diet for all

Although each person's fertility status is unique, eating a healthy, balanced diet is thought to aid fertility, and continues to be important once pregnant. Some research suggests that following the Mediterranean model of eating (see pp.10–13) is not only beneficial in pregnancy but may also reduce the risk of fertility problems by up to 66 per cent. Studies indicate that unhealthy diets, rich in red and processed meats and foods with trans fats, crisps, sweets, and sweetened beverages can have negative effects on fertility. Some studies have found links that suggest a high consumption of fast food and eating only small amounts of fruit may increase the time it takes to get pregnant. More specifically, other studies suggest that couples who eat fish and seafood regularly become pregnant sooner than those who consume fewer than two servings of fish a week.

Nutrients for women and men

In the US, a study following over 116,000 women found that higher fertility rates in women were associated with diets rich in monounsaturated fats – found in foods such as olives, avocados, and nuts and seeds – and based on vegetable proteins rather than animal proteins, and fibre-rich carbohydrates. Other reviews into past studies found that, for women trying to become pregnant naturally, folic acid, vitamin B12, omega-3 fatty acids, and Mediterranean-style diets were linked to increased fertility.

For men, while many factors can affect fertility, a diet that includes omega-3 fatty acids found in foods such as oily fish is thought to be particularly important for sperm quality and quantity, while saturated and trans fats may be detrimental.

Couples receiving fertility treatments may be more likely to conceive where women take folic acid supplements and eat a diet high in isoflavones (plant-based oestrogens with antioxidant activity) such as soya, and men eat an antioxidant-rich diet.

Welcome
to pregnancy

Your body is working overtime in pregnancy to help your little one grow and provide a comfortable home for them over the next nine months. During this crucial period, pregnancy hormones cause your body to go through a whole raft of changes, such as loosened joints and ligaments and larger breasts, and you may experience a range of symptoms. You may veer from feeling excitement one moment to being filled with worry, especially when it comes to looking after your body and your baby. All of these changes can make this time of transition a challenging one that's often underestimated.

The following chapter provides an overview of pregnancy, looking at the key changes your body goes through, right up until the birth, and how your baby grows and develops. It also takes you through the first precious twelve weeks with your newborn – known as the fourth trimester – when rest and recuperation are so imperative. Common pregnancy symptoms are explored, together with nutritional and lifestyle tips for coping and advice on when to seek medical support. Topics such as eating in labour and your nutritional needs while breastfeeding are also discussed. Understanding what is happening to your body and your baby now can help you to cope with pregnancy stressors and enjoy this precious and incredible journey.

The first trimester

Congratulations if you have just discovered you are pregnant! Once you see a positive pregnancy test you are likely to be about four weeks pregnant already, since your pregnancy is dated from the first day of your last period. In this first trimester – the initial 13 weeks of pregnancy – your baby grows rapidly and your body is already experiencing some significant changes.

What's happening to you now?

In the first trimester, your body is undergoing a number of changes and you may experience a range of symptoms (see pp.32–37), many of which are due to the rising levels of certain hormones.

- **Your blood volume increases** and your heart pumps more blood around the body to support you and your growing baby.
- **Your breasts may feel sore and tender** thanks to hormonal surges (see below). They also enlarge as milk glands and tissues build up, preparing them to make the most nutritious possible milk for your baby.
- **Common symptoms** now include nausea, fatigue, and constipation.

How hormones affect your body in pregnancy

The main pregnancy-related hormones are produced in the ovaries and the placenta, the temporary organ that develops during pregnancy (see opposite). These hormones support the development of your baby and how you adapt to them can determine the symptoms you experience, with some women being more sensitive to these hormonal shifts.

- **Human chorionic gonadotropin (hCG)** is the hormone detected on your home pregnancy test. Its primary role is to ensure that progesterone production continues in pregnancy. Both hCG and thyroid hormone are thought to contribute to pregnancy nausea and sickness (see pp.32–34), most common in the first trimester when hCG

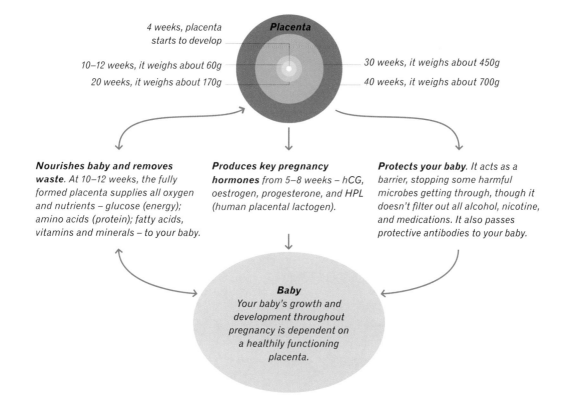

4 weeks, placenta starts to develop

10–12 weeks, it weighs about 60g

20 weeks, it weighs about 170g

Placenta

30 weeks, it weighs about 450g

40 weeks, it weighs about 700g

Nourishes baby and removes waste. At 10–12 weeks, the fully formed placenta supplies all oxygen and nutrients – glucose (energy); amino acids (protein); fatty acids, vitamins and minerals – to your baby.

Produces key pregnancy hormones from 5–8 weeks – hCG, oestrogen, progesterone, and HPL (human placental lactogen).

Protects your baby. It acts as a barrier, stopping some harmful microbes getting through, though it doesn't filter out all alcohol, nicotine, and medications. It also passes protective antibodies to your baby.

Baby
Your baby's growth and development throughout pregnancy is dependent on a healthily functioning placenta.

Your baby's life support

The placenta exchanges nutrients, gases, and waste via a complex network of blood vessels. As it grows throughout pregnancy, its ever-increasing surface area ensures it has the capacity to support your baby right up until the birth.

levels are at their highest. HCG is also thought to be responsible for the urge to urinate frequently in the first trimester.

- **Oestrogen and progesterone**, produced in a normal menstrual cycle, rise considerably in pregnancy. Though essential for pregnancy, they can cause side effects such as mood swings, which are common in the first trimester as your body adapts. Progesterone also slows down muscle movement in the body, which impacts digestion, slowing the bowels, which can lead to constipation. High progesterone levels are also partly responsible for sore, tender breasts. Oestrogen, together with relaxin, relaxes the blood vessels, allowing more blood to be circulated, which contributes to an increased need to urinate and can make you feel warmer.

What's happening to your baby?

Your baby grows rapidly in the first trimester and by the end of this time will weigh around 28g (1oz). The limbs have formed and the major body systems and organs are also starting to form.

The second trimester

The second trimester of pregnancy spans from weeks 14 to 27. Some women find that symptoms such as nausea come and go still, but for many, early pregnancy symptoms subside as the body adjusts to pregnancy hormones, and the majority of women find this trimester a lot easier to manage.

What's happening to you now?

As your body adjusts to the pregnancy hormones and these also start to stabilize, you are likely to find that any nausea and fatigue you experienced in the first trimester recedes and your energy levels return to normal. Many women feel revitalized and find that the second trimester is one of the most enjoyable parts of their pregnancy.

During this trimester, though many of the unwelcome symptoms of early pregnancy disappear or lessen, you may experience some new challenges, often related to your growing bump. This is also an exciting time when you start to feel your baby move and the pregnancy begins to feel very real.

- **As nausea subsides**, you are likely to find that your appetite increases. If you were able to eat bland foods only in the first trimester, now is the time to replenish your nutrients. If you can, try to eat a nutrient-rich diet with vegetables, fruit, and other healthy fibres, proteins, and healthy fats (see pp.40–57). If you are still concerned about nutrient intake, continue with a pregnancy supplement (see p.58).
- **Your abdomen starts to expand** as your uterus grows and begins to push upwards. By around 20 weeks, your bump may start to be visible. As the uterus moves up, this can relieve pressure on your bladder and you may urinate less frequently.
- **You feel your baby move for the first time**. At around 18 weeks for a first pregnancy and a bit earlier for subsequent ones, you will feel the first flutterings as your baby continues to grow and gain in strength.

- **You may experience dizziness** or lightheadedness as the increased blood flow to your baby can lower blood pressure (see p.37). Take things slowly if you feel lightheaded and stay hydrated and nourished. If you are concerned, talk to your midwife or healthcare provider.
- **You may experience aching**, including back ache, as your increasing weight adds to the strain on your body. Exercise gently and practise pelvic floor exercises regularly to strengthen your pelvic muscles.
- **Stretch marks** may appear on your stomach, breasts, thighs, or buttocks. You may also experience other skin changes; for example, the skin around your nipples may darken, or patches of darker skin pigmentation may appear elsewhere on your body, which affects all skin tones and is caused by pregnancy hormones.
- **Your skin may feel itchy.** Pregnancy hormones can dry your skin, making it more prone to itching, and your skin stretches considerably as your bump grows, which can cause or exacerbate itching. If itching is severe, seek medical advice as this may indicate a more serious condition known as cholestasis.
- **You may experience swelling** in your ankles or hands, known as oedema (see p.37). Increased fluids in pregnancy and a slower circulation can cause fluid to build up. Stay well hydrated to help flush out excess fluids, exercise regularly to keep your circulation moving (see p.62), and take time to rest and put your feet up.
- **Your gums may feel soft** and bleed more easily due to pregnancy hormones. Visit your dentist and practise good dental hygiene.

What's happening to your baby?

In the second trimester, your baby grows larger and becomes stronger. By the end of this trimester, they will weigh around 900g (2lb) and measure about 36cm (14in). Your baby's organs will be fully formed, though they are still developing, and a fine covering of hair appears over the skin. Your baby also starts to hear in this trimester and begins to swallow. Later on in this trimester, your baby will begin to move around more and will start to establish a sleeping and waking cycle. You may begin to notice this as your baby becomes more active or settles down at regular times of the day or night.

The third trimester

This trimester comprises weeks 28 until the birth, at around 40 weeks. For some, this can be an immensely challenging time, physically and emotionally, as the growing bump increases the demands on the body and thoughts about the birth surface. It can also be a time of overwhelming excitement as you anticipate meeting your baby.

What's happening to you now?

As your bump grows ever bigger and your body prepares for the birth, you may find earlier symptoms returning or new ones arising. Staying well nourished and hydrated is key now.

- **Heartburn and indigestion** (see p.35) may return or arise now. As your uterus pushes your stomach upwards, stomach acids can be forced into the oesophagus, causing the burning sensation known as acid reflux. You may also feel bloated and nauseous.
- **Pelvic girdle pain** can worsen in the third trimester. This can cause pain in the pubic and groin area, the lower back, and down into the thighs, and you may experience clicking in the pelvic area. Talk to your healthcare provider about how to manage this symptom. You may need a support belt, combined with rest and gentle stretches, and should take care moving and lifting.
- **A range of other factors** can affect how you feel in this trimester. Sleep may be more challenging (see p.64) and, together with the demands on your body, lead to fatigue. Swelling in the joints and feet may worsen, which needs monitoring as this can be an early sign of pre-eclampsia. You may also experience leg cramps, and problems such as haemorrhoids (piles) and varicose veins may develop (see p.37). After about 33 weeks, you may start to experience Braxton Hicks' contractions, which are practice contractions for labour.

- **Your appetite may increase or dip**. To fuel your baby's growth and prepare nutritionally for the birth and beyond, you need about an extra 200 calories a day (see p.46), but no more, depending on how active you are. Your baby's body will begin to store minerals such as calcium and iron so you need a sufficient intake of these nutrients. Research suggests that up to 72 per cent of women are low in iron in the third trimester, resulting in anaemia, linked to low or high birth weights. Your midwife or healthcare provider will monitor your levels and discuss supplements if needed (see p.58). It's advisable to continue with folic acid and vitamin D supplements. If symptoms make eating a balanced, Mediterranean-style diet a challenge, a general pregnancy supplement may be best. As well as supplements, focus on food sources of key nutrients (see pp.52–56).

What's happening to your baby?

Your baby is growing rapidly now and by the birth will weigh on average around 3.5kg (7lb 7oz) – about the size of a watermelon – and will measure about 51cm (20in) long. The lungs are fully formed by the end of this trimester, ready for your baby to start breathing in the outside world, and your baby's bones, made up of cartilage, continue to harden, though these will carry on developing up until early adulthood.

Getting ready for the birth and your baby

Work on breathing exercises to help you relax and to use as a tool in labour. Sleeping on your side is important, too (see p.65), and ensure that any exercise you do doesn't strain your body (see p.62). Try low-impact exercises such as pregnancy yoga or Pilates and walking, and keep active. Practising pelvic floor exercises is key now to strengthen the pelvic muscles and avoid problems such as stress incontinence after the birth.

When your baby arrives, time to cook may be scarce. Stock up on storecupboard basics such as pasta, rice, tinned fish, and nut butters, and batch cook and freeze sauces and bases for rice and pasta dishes for easy, nutritious meals after the birth. You can also freeze toppings, pre-sliced bread, and fruit such as bananas and berries (which are easy to whip into a smoothie). If you wish, stock up on some good-quality ready meals, too, and get nutritious snacks, such as oatcakes, ginger biscuits, and dried fruit, ready to fuel you when you're feeding your baby.

Eating during labour

Your body works incredibly hard during labour, especially in advanced labour as you approach the birth. Your uterus is mostly made up of muscle tissues. As muscles contract they use up energy, so your body needs to provide nutrients to meet these energy needs.

Very little research has been done into the specific nutritional needs of women during labour, but a review of the studies available found that when women laboured with few, or no, restrictions on eating and drinking, they had shorter labours by around 16 minutes. Organizations such as the World Health Organization (WHO) recommend that women who are thought to be at low-risk of interventions such as epidurals or operative births should feel free to eat and drink as normal in labour.

Most women tend to lose their appetite gradually as labour progresses, and some may even vomit. This is likely to be caused by the gastrointestinal tract slowing down as the body directs its energy to the uterus for the birth. It's a good idea, therefore, to fuel your body in the lead up to labour and in the early stages to ensure that you have the energy needed to sustain you throughout labour and birth (see opposite).

Certain drugs, for example opiates such as pethidine, or entonox (gas and air), can make you feel nauseous and may affect your appetite during labour. Anti-sickness medication can be given with opiates to reduce nausea, while the effects of entonox are short-term so any sickness usually passes quickly. Less commonly, epidurals may also cause nausea, but again, anti-sickness medication can help to reduce this feeling. If you do find that the effects of pain relief reduce your desire to eat, ensure that you stay hydrated and, if possible, see if you can manage plain snacks such as oatcakes.

When labour is complicated

If your pregnancy has been high-risk and you have a greater chance of a Caesarean under general anaesthetic, eating in labour can increase your risk of experiencing breathing difficulties during the birth. Each woman's circumstances are unique. If there are concerns about your labour and birth, talk to your midwife or healthcare provider about whether it's best to avoid eating in labour after a certain point and discuss strategies for fuelling labour, such as eating well in the build up.

1st stage of labour: latent phase. As the cervix softens and starts to dilate, you experience irregular contractions.

1st stage of labour: established. Contractions are regular now as the cervix continues to dilate.

Late 1st stage/ 2nd stage of labour. The cervix dilates fully and your baby is born.

3rd stage of labour. Placenta is delivered.

1st stage: *latent phase*

• *Eat and drink as usual now. Have smaller, more frequent meals. Try complex carbs, such as pasta; sandwiches; toast with spread; pitta; nuts; seeds; fruit; veg; popcorn; and energy bars. Opt for isotonic drinks to balance salt and sugar levels or water. Avoid caffeine.*
Why? *To fuel labour and stay well hydrated.*

1st stage: *established*

• *Continue to snack, unless you feel nauseous, and stay hydrated. Try smaller bites such as sandwiches, fruit, toast, pitta, nuts, seeds, or even a teaspoon of honey. Avoid fatty foods, which can worsen nausea. Sip fluids to stay hydrated.*
Why? *To sustain energy. Getting dehydrated now can affect the baby's heartbeat.*

Late 1st stage/2nd stage

• *You are unlikely to want to eat now and may even vomit – whether or not you eat – closer to delivery. Sip fluids to stay hydrated.*
Why? *Digestion slows down as energy is focused on the uterus. Intense contractions focus you wholly on the birth of your baby now.*

3rd stage

• *Staying hydrated now is key. About an hour after delivery you may feel very hungry. Try eating complex carbs and/or dark chocolate.*
Why? *Blood is lost during the birth so hydration replaces fluids and supports circulation.*

Eating in labour

The illustration above provides a guide to eating and drinking during the stages of a low-risk labour and delivery. In certain situations, you may be advised to avoid food and/ or fluids (see opposite).

Bear in mind the following when planning how to meet your energy needs during labour.

• **In pregnancy, when possible**, focus on eating a highly nutritious diet (see pp.40–57) to build stores for your body in the lead up to labour.

• **Keep well hydrated** throughout pregnancy and particularly as you go into labour. Being dehydrated in labour can affect your baby's heartbeat. Although this can be easily treated with oral or IV fluids, sipping isotonic drinks or water regularly can prevent this in the first place. Avoid caffeine in labour as well as fizzy drinks and orange juice, whose acidity can cause nausea.

• **Listen to your body in labour** and avoid forcing yourself to eat, but do try to keep hydrated. As you sip on drinks, make sure you keep emptying your bladder, too, to create space for your baby in the pelvis and hopefully ensure they are in a good position for the birth.

The fourth trimester

The 12-week period after the birth is known as the fourth trimester. Before the birth, your focus is likely to be on a safe delivery and ensuring that your newborn is healthy and content. While birth can feel empowering for some, it can also take a toll on your mental and physical health, so support is key now.

What's happening to you now?

If you had medication in labour, once it has worn off you may still be in substantial pain, and some women need to continue with pain relief at home. Uterine contractions that feel like strong cramps continue for several days after birth, to help the uterus contract down to its original size. Breastfeeding triggers these contractions and they may be more noticeable while feeding. Hormones fluctuate once again, with oestrogen and progesterone falling and the milk-making hormone, prolactin, rising. You may be very tired as you recover from the birth and adjust to night-time feeding.

Recuperating after the birth

It can take weeks, months, or, for some women, longer to recover fully physically and emotionally after labour. However, if you're experiencing pain after three months, talk to a healthcare advisor as this needs investigating. For some, recovery is especially hard. In the UK, it's thought that around 30,000 women a year experience PTSD symptoms post-birth, such as flashbacks and increased anxiety. This can be the case, for example, if a birth didn't go to plan and/or medical interventions were needed. Moreover, in the COVID-19 pandemic, many women felt isolated after labour, often coping without the support of a partner during their hospital stay.

A strong support network and allowing time for recovery post-birth is crucial. Traditionally in the West, a rest period of three to four weeks was the norm after giving birth to allow mothers to recuperate. Now, the emphasis seems to have shifted to recovering quickly and resuming caring roles, even while facing physical and mental challenges and trying to establish breastfeeding. In many Eastern cultures, there's still a prescribed period of time to focus on recovery. Where possible, family and friends care for the mother, and often her family and home, leaving her to rest, stay nourished, and focus on her baby. Seek support now and rest as much as possible.

Coping with the baby blues

In the week following birth, your body goes through huge and swift hormonal and chemical changes. Sudden drops in progesterone and oestrogen can leave you feeling low or mildly depressed. Around 60–80 per cent of women experience the "baby blues", often starting in the first three days and lasting for a couple of weeks. You may feel anxious; restless; tearful; irritable; prone to mood swings; for a first child, nervous about motherhood; and struggle to sleep. Keep an eye on how you feel, perhaps keeping a journal if this helps.

Recognizing post-natal depression

If the baby blues continue beyond two weeks, this may be a sign that you're suffering with post-natal depression (PND), which affects 10–15 per cent of mothers. PND often starts within two months of the birth, though it can begin several months later. You may feel low, hopeless, anxious, and struggle to bond with your baby, which can leave you feeling guilty and self-critical. In addition, your appetite may wane, you may find it hard to care for yourself and your baby, and struggle to find enjoyment in life.

The good news is that with support, PND can be treated and you're most likely to develop a nurturing, fulfilling bond with your baby. It is crucial, therefore, to seek support if worried about your mental or emotional health. Try to talk openly to someone you trust and recruit professional help.

Feeding your baby in the early weeks

You may choose to breastfeed exclusively, combine breast and formula, or formula feed exclusively. Breast milk is the ideal first food, providing all the nutrients your baby needs in the first six months (apart from vitamin D, which breastfed babies need a supplement of); tailored antibodies to help your baby fight infection; and hormones to support growth and development. Formula milk is also designed to supply the key nutrients your baby needs.

If you plan to breastfeed, prepare before the birth. Antenatal groups hold breastfeeding sessions; online classes, support groups, and professionals on social media can help; and chat to friends and family who breastfed.

In the first days after the birth your milk contains colostrum. This thick, yellow–golden milk is produced in tiny amounts, perfectly tailored for your newborn's energy needs. It contains antibodies and is high in vitamins A, D, and B12 to help build the immune system. Typically, two to four days after the birth, colostrum transitions to mature milk. Milk production now changes from being controlled solely by your hormones to being determined mainly by supply and demand – when your baby suckles, this signals the breasts to make more milk, so you constantly meet your baby's needs. There are plenty of ways to help feeding go smoothly.

- **Enjoy skin-to-skin contact** straight after the birth and as much as possible in the early days. This close contact is thought to help establish breastfeeding and is associated with longer breastfeeding rates.
- **Find a position that works for you both**, ensuring your baby is well latched on. If you experience prolonged pain (longer than 30 seconds) when feeding and/or have damaged nipples, this suggests that your baby isn't latched on properly, so seek qualified breastfeeding support.
- **Check your baby makes a swallowing action** when feeding. This, together with meeting their weight milestones and producing wet and dirty nappies, indicates they are feeding well.
- **Feed responsively**. Whenever your baby cries or roots for the nipple, offer a feed, even if they have only just finished one. Your baby may be going through one of their frequent growth spurts, so feeding on demand ensures that your milk production increases to meet their needs. Avoid offering a dummy or supplementing with formula.
- **Feed your baby frequently**. Newborns typically feed every 1–3 hours, with an average of 10–12 feeds over 24 hours. Offer both breasts at feeds to ensure they get all the milk they need. Newborns can be very sleepy. If your baby isn't waking regularly to feed, rouse them at least every three hours. If they fall asleep at the breast or after the first breast, remove them, change their nappy to increase their alertness, then offer the other breast. Try compressing your breast manually, as if expressing, during feeds to stimulate milk flow and trigger your baby to suck.
- **Stay hydrated**. Breastfeeding is thirsty work so keep water nearby.

Protein 70g a day

45g

+ 25g

Protein is needed to produce breast milk and aids your recovery post-birth. **Sources include** *lean red meat, fish, poultry, beans, pulses, dairy, and tofu.*

Omega-3 1.3g a day

1.1g

+ 200mg

Essential omega-3s, especially DHA, support your baby's brain development when breastfeeding and there's some evidence they reduces allergies. **Sources include** *oily fish (limit to 2 portions a week), flaxseeds, walnuts, and soya beans.*

Calcium 1250mg a day

700mg

+ 550mg

A calcium deficiency is more likely when breastfeeding so it's advisable to increase your intake. **Sources include** *dairy, soya, whole sardines, broccoli, and fortified food.*

Folate 260mcg a day

200mcg

+ 60mcg

Needed for the healthy development of your baby's red blood cells. **Sources include** *spinach, lean beef, black-eyed beans, rice, asparagus, and fortified foods.*

Choline 550mcg a day

425mcg

+ 125mcg

This plays an important role in your baby's brain development. **Sources include** *lean beef, eggs, salmon, pork, chicken, almonds, and broccoli.*

Iodine 290mcg a day

150mcg

+ 140mcg

Needed to create thyroid hormones to aid your baby's brain development. **Sources include** *dairy, white fish, and eggs. Avoid seaweed – its very high iodine levels can lead to an overactive thyroid.*

Nutrient needs while breastfeeding

As well as needing extra calories when breastfeeding (see p.46), you need more of certain nutrients (see right) to aid milk production, deliver nutrients to your baby, and support recovery. It's also important to keep your iron intake up to replace any lost at birth, and to eat plenty of fibre to avoid constipation, common after birth. If your diet does not fulfil your nutrient needs, supplements may be needed (see p.58).

Approximate average daily intake needed for women if not breastfeeding

Approximate additional nutrient needs when breastfeeding

How you might be feeling

Pregnancy can be a challenging time for many women. Alongside the demands of growing a baby, women can experience a range of symptoms, including common complaints such as nausea, fatigue, and constipation. Knowing what to expect and how to manage symptoms can help to make pregnancy as comfortable as possible.

Nausea and vomiting

Around 80 to 90 per cent of women suffer with nausea in pregnancy, with 60 to 70 per cent of these also vomiting. Nausea is thought to be caused by pregnancy hormones – in particular, human chorionic gonadotropin (hCG) – which increase rapidly in early pregnancy (see p.20). Some women feel nausea on waking, explaining the term "morning sickness", but the vast majority find nausea can hit at any time of the day. For most, nausea eases at around 16 to 20 weeks. Symptoms can vary and include:

- **Nausea**, which can be occasional or fairly constant. It may be accompanied by dry retching – the feeling you will vomit, but without being sick. For some, sensitivity to smells or the sight of certain foods triggers nausea.
- **Vomiting**, which can be occasional or fairly frequent and can temporarily relieve nausea.
- **In two per cent of pregnancies**, nausea and vomiting is severe and prolonged, a condition known as hyperemesis gravidarum. This makes it hard to keep down fluids or food, causing weight loss, which can lead to malnourishment and dehydration. Specialist treatment, sometimes in hospital, may be needed. It is vital to talk to your healthcare provider if you have extreme sickness. Research suggests that this affects quality of life in pregnancy and can make women less willing to fall pregnant again. Getting medical help, having a support network, and trying to stay as comfortable as possible is key for your health and happiness.

Adding a little ginger to foods and infusions is an effective remedy for nausea.

What you can do

Try the following to take the edge off nausea.

- **Get outside**. Fresh air and natural light can help to reduce nausea.
- **Avoid strong smells**. If kitchen or cooking smells make you feel sick, enlist help in the kitchen whenever possible.
- **Build in relaxation time**. Stress and anxiety can exacerbate nausea. Get enough sleep and take time to rest. Try practising relaxation exercises such as deep breathing.
- **Eat little and often**. Try five to six small meals a day. Some women find that eating a plain snack, such as a cracker, before getting up each morning helps to settle the stomach first thing.
- **Avoid high-fat or spicy foods**, which can exacerbate nausea.
- **Try ginger root tea**. Ginger is an effective remedy for nausea, but limit your intake to less than 3g of raw ginger per day.
- **Opt for a bland diet short term** if you can't face lots of vegetables, but keep your protein intake up and take supplements. You need to ensure that what you eat provides energy for you and your baby. Reassuringly, a simple meal of bread and eggs has many key nutrients (see below).

Egg and bread nutrition

If you can manage only bland foods, fortified white bread and an egg provide several key nutrients. If you can manage it, 50:50 white/ wholemeal bread will up your fibre intake.

RI = reference intake. This is the amount of calories and nutrients to aim for daily. Bear in mind that in pregnancy, your need for some nutrients increases (see pp.48–57).

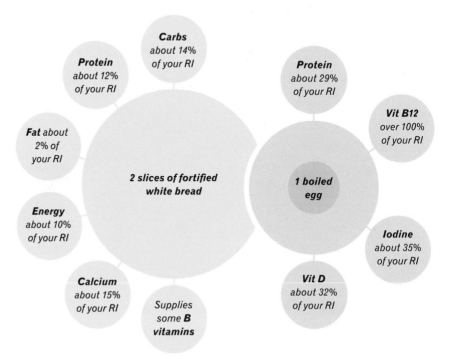

Carbs about 14% of your RI

Protein about 12% of your RI

Protein about 29% of your RI

Vit B12 over 100% of your RI

Fat about 2% of your RI

2 slices of fortified white bread

1 boiled egg

Energy about 10% of your RI

Iodine about 35% of your RI

Calcium about 15% of your RI

Supplies some **B** vitamins

Vit D about 32% of your RI

Heartburn and indigestion

Pregnancy hormones relax the valve between the oesophagus and stomach. This means stomach acid can leak into the oesophagus, causing heartburn and indigestion. Later in pregnancy, your enlarged uterus may press on the stomach, which can leave you feeling full and bloated, burpy, sick, sometimes bringing up food, and/or with a heart-burning sensation. While extremely unpleasant and painful, this is not serious.

What you can do

Try the following suggestions to help relieve the discomfort.

- **Eat small, frequent meals**, rather than two to three larger meals a day.
- **Aim to have a three-hour gap** between your last meal and bedtime.
- **Sit upright when eating** to help take pressure off your stomach.
- **Avoid spicy and fried foods**, as well as citrus fruits and chocolate, all of which can lead to heartburn.
- **Try drinking a glass of milk** to help ease heartburn.
- **Sleep in a more upright position** with supportive pillows.
- **Stop smoking and avoid alcohol** if you haven't done so already.
- **If heartburn is chronic**, consider consulting a trained nutritionist to see if individually tailored dietary interventions can help.

Constipation and diarrhoea

High progesterone levels can slow the movement of food through the digestive tract, causing constipation, which affects 11 to 38 per cent of pregnant women. Constipation is also common post-birth, caused by hormonal shifts and sometimes labour medication. For some, pregnancy hormones cause diarrhoea. In this case, talk to a healthcare professional as digestive changes can impact your nutrient status in pregnancy.

What you can do

The following tips can help to reduce digestive complaints.

- **To prevent or relieve constipation**, include lots of fibre in your diet – aim for 25 to 28g (about 1oz) a day. Choose wholegrains, pulses, and fruit and vegetables. If needed, you may also want to consider a fibre supplement, such as psyllium, wheat bran, or oat bran, adding 1 to 2 tablespoons a day to your cereal.

- **Drink plenty of fluids** (ideally water) – aim for between 2 and 2.5 litres (3½ and 3¾ pints) a day (see p.42).
- **Keep active**. Opt for gentle activities such as yoga and swimming and walk more to keep the circulation and digestion moving.
- **Iron supplements** can worsen or cause constipation. If taking these, talk to your healthcare provider to discuss other solutions and/or dosage.
- **If lifestyle interventions do not help**, monitored occasional or short-term laxatives may be advised by your doctor or a registered dietitian to avoid dehydration and electrolyte imbalances. Never take laxatives without consulting a health professional.

Fatigue

In early pregnancy, levels of sleep-promoting progesterone rise sharply, which can cause extreme tiredness. Your blood volume also increases to supply the developing placenta and fetal circulation, and your heart pumps faster and stronger, increasing pulse and breathing rates, which adds to tiredness. Later in pregnancy, low iron levels can cause fatigue. Ultimately, fatigue is a signal to slow down and respect that your body is going through the strenuous and life-changing task of growing your baby.

What you can do to cope with fatigue

Try the following measures to renew your energy.

- **Rest as much as possible**. Don't feel guilty about resting, especially in the third trimester when fatigue can return, exacerbated by interrupted nighttime sleep.
- **Try to stay active**. Stretch, move around, and have a walk in the fresh air each day, all of which will help increase energy levels.
- **Keep hydrated** (see p.42). Try to drink the majority of your fluid intake towards the start of the day and sip small amounts in the hours before bedtime to avoid or limit nighttime waking.
- **Eat a healthy, balanced diet**, opting for small, more frequent meals to sustain energy. Reduce caffeine (see p.61) to avoid energy spikes and dips. Take supplements, too, to ensure you get key nutrients (see p.58).
- **Practise good sleep hygiene** (see p.64). Limit screen time before bed, try to sleep in a cool, dark room, and wind down prior to sleeping. Consider investing in a pregnancy pillow to help you get comfortable.

Other symptoms

Some pregnancy symptoms may need monitoring or medical attention.

- **Pelvic girdle pain (PGP)** causes pain in the pelvis and groin area, making movement hard. Rest is key and treatment may be needed.
- **Dizziness** may signal a drop in blood pressure, low blood sugar, or low iron levels. Your healthcare provider can check this and monitor you.
- **Backache** is common in pregnancy. Stay active and if it continues, consult your healthcare provider, who may refer you for physiotherapy.
- **Headaches** can be more frequent in pregnancy. Seek medical advice if these are chronic or severe.
- **Swelling (oedema)** is caused by extra fluids in the body, often in the feet and legs. Consult your healthcare provider, rest, and stay hydrated.
- **Varicose veins and haemorrhoids** (piles) can be a concern in pregnancy. Stay active, rest, and drink plenty of fluids. Your healthcare provider can monitor you and prescribe treatments to relieve haemorrhoid discomfort.
- **Leg cramps**, especially at night, are caused by pregnancy hormones. Stay hydrated and try stretching your calves for relief. Seek advice if severe.

Cravings

Some pregnant women experience a strong desire to eat a certain food. While cravings don't cause physical discomfort, they can mean you need to keep an eye on your nutrient intake. Research suggests that, of those who experience cravings, around 40 per cent crave sweet foods, 33 per cent salty foods, 17 per cent seek spicy foods, and 10 per cent crave citrus and sour flavours. One theory is that there is an evolutionary reason as the body signals which vitamins and minerals are missing for the fetus. However, as few cravings are for the healthiest foods, this is unlikely.

What you can do

- **Consider emotional hunger versus physical hunger**. Pregnancy can be tough and food can comfort and soothe, so check in on how you're feeling.
- **Be aware of what your body is saying**, but resist always giving in to cravings, as your diet during pregnancy needs to be varied to provide all the nutrients that your growing baby needs every day (see p.40).
- **If you crave non-food items**, speak to your healthcare provider as this is a sign of an eating disorder called "pica".

Nutrition and lifestyle
for pregnancy

Pregnancy can be a time of uncertainty and confusion when it comes to your diet – how much should you eat, what should you eat, and which foods should you definitely avoid? It is clear, though, that what you eat before and during pregnancy can positively impact your health in pregnancy. It's also increasingly understood that your diet has implications for your baby's health both during pregnancy and in future years.

The following section looks at the key nutrients for a healthy pregnancy, together with their food sources; explores the important role of supplements – especially when nausea means you are struggling to eat a varied diet – and explains why good hydration is crucial now. Taking control of your diet is one significant way you can optimize your health and wellbeing in pregnancy and give your baby the very best nutritional start.

In addition to eating well, a whole-lifestyle approach is explored. The importance of staying active to keep you strong and heart healthy during pregnancy is discussed, as is the role of sleep hygiene to help you sleep as soundly as possible. Practical guidance and tips reassure you on how to exercise safely and optimize sleep quality and duration. As an evidence-based nutritionist, I can also see the benefit of sometimes taking a holistic approach to help you manage the ups and downs of pregnancy and promote the wellbeing of you and your baby.

A nourishing pregnancy

Good nutrition in pregnancy is vital for you and your baby. You need to ensure that you are consuming enough energy to support you and your growing baby's needs, while the nutrients your body stores support your baby's development and help to reduce the risk of health complications arising in your baby.

Food and supplements in pregnancy

Getting the right amount of essential nutrients is vital in pregnancy. While a "foods first" approach is important – eating a balanced diet with a range of nutrients – supplements are often needed (see p.58), especially if nausea means you're struggling to eat a varied diet. Taking supplements doesn't mean that you don't need to worry about what you eat; you should still optimize your diet to give you and your baby the best nutritional outcome.

Your pregnancy diet

Eating healthily in pregnancy helps to optimize your and your baby's health; enables you to manage symptoms such as constipation; and supports your energy needs. Moreover, what you eat in pregnancy is thought to influence your baby's health up to their second birthday (see p.44).

Aim to model a Mediterranean-style diet, following the guidelines on page 13. Eat a wide variety of foods from the main food groups, including starchy and fibrous foods such as bread, rice, and potatoes; protein and calcium sources; and plenty of vegetables and fruits. You need a bit more protein and calcium in pregnancy and when breastfeeding. You also need to increase your intake of some other key nutrients (see p.31 for your breastfeeding needs, and pp.48–57 for key pregnancy nutrients). If symptoms such as nausea make a varied diet feel unachievable, rest assured that many bland foods supply key nutrients. When you feel able, return to a balanced diet with lots of colourful produce.

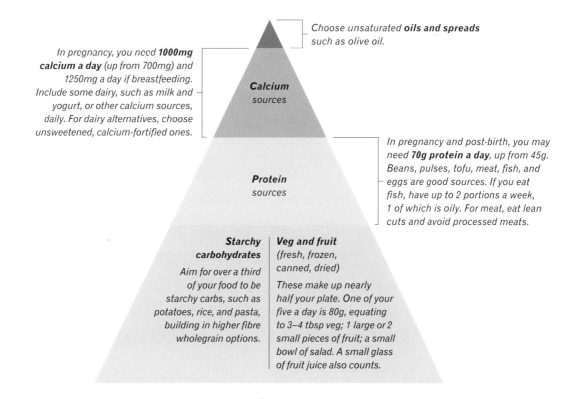

In pregnancy, you need **1000mg calcium a day** (up from 700mg) and 1250mg a day if breastfeeding. Include some dairy, such as milk and yogurt, or other calcium sources, daily. For dairy alternatives, choose unsweetened, calcium-fortified ones.

Choose unsaturated **oils and spreads** such as olive oil.

Calcium sources

In pregnancy and post-birth, you may need **70g protein a day**, up from 45g. Beans, pulses, tofu, meat, fish, and eggs are good sources. If you eat fish, have up to 2 portions a week, 1 of which is oily. For meat, eat lean cuts and avoid processed meats.

Protein sources

Starchy carbohydrates

Aim for over a third of your food to be starchy carbs, such as potatoes, rice, and pasta, building in higher fibre wholegrain options.

Veg and fruit (fresh, frozen, canned, dried)

These make up nearly half your plate. One of your five a day is 80g, equating to 3–4 tbsp veg; 1 large or 2 small pieces of fruit; a small bowl of salad. A small glass of fruit juice also counts.

A balanced pregnancy diet

Guidelines advise that over two-thirds of your food should be made up of fruit, veg, and other complex carbs. The rest of your plate should be made up of protein and calcium sources, both of which you need more of now.

Why gut health is important in pregnancy

Gut health is an exciting new area of nutritional science, as we find links between our minds and gut via the brain–gut axis and discover the role of healthy gut bacteria in immunity and mental health. Gut bacteria aid mineral absorption, synthesize vitamins, and digest fibre, strengthening the gut and helping the liver to regulate blood sugars and appetite. It's thought maternal diet and gut bacteria may play a role in babies' developing gut microbiomes. In pregnancy, a Mediterranean-style diet with a variety of produce, fibre, complex carbs, and healthy fats; fermented foods such as yogurt and kimchi, which contain probiotics – healthy live bacteria; and foods such as apples, prunes, pears, leeks, garlic, and pulses that contain prebiotics, which feed existing healthy bacteria, can all benefit your baby's health. Babies also receive maternal bacteria in vaginal births (research into transferring vaginal bacteria to Caesarean-born babies is ongoing), and there are chances to optimize babies' gut bacteria with breastfeeding and weaning.

Staying hydrated in pregnancy

Hydration is essential for our health at all times and is especially key in pregnancy. Water ensures that nutrients and oxygen are carried through the blood to our cells and that our kidneys can filter and excrete waste. In pregnancy, your fluid needs increase, to support your increased blood volume (and in turn your baby and placenta) and to make up for fluid

*In pregnancy, aim to drink **2–2.5 litres (3½–3¾ pints), or 8–10 cups, of water or other healthy fluids a day**.*

Good sources of hydration

Water

*Water can make up all of your fluid intake, or aim for at least **5–6 glasses a day** (1 glass on waking; 1 glass with each meal and snack; and sips throughout the day).*

Safe herbal teas

*Enjoy **1–2 cups**. Avoid experimenting now or drinking too much of one tea. Stick to ginger, chamomile, lemon, peppermint, or rooibos. Avoid raspberry leaf tea before 32 weeks as it may stimuate the uterus.*

Milk

Both dairy and plant-based milks are hydrating. You may wish to choose semi-skimmed milk to keep saturated fat intake low.

Fruit juices

*Juice hydrates and its nutrients add to your five-a-day quota. However, have no more than **1 small glass of 150ml (5fl oz) a day** to avoid excess sugar.*

Sources of hydration

Water is the best hydrator, but other drinks can count towards your fluid intake, too, as shown in this diagram.

Limit or avoid these drinks

Drinks with sugar

Limit sugar-sweetened drinks, such as squash, as the sugar adds up. If you regularly drink squash, opt for sugar-free or make your own fruit-infused water.

Flavoured drinks

Flavoured waters, milks, and "juice" drinks can contain too much sugar on top of your dietary intake for the day so limit these.

Fizzy drinks

Fizzy drinks can contain both sugar and caffeine (see above and below). If you like fizzy drinks, try carbonated water or add fizzy water to sugar-free squash or juice.

Caffeine drinks

*Mildly diuretic, tea and coffee do hydrate, but in pregnancy, avoid caffeine or limit to **200mg** a day (see p.61). Per cup, white tea has up to 60mg; black tea up to 90mg; green tea up to 45 mg (Matcha up to 35mg per ½ tsp powder); and coffee up to 100mg.*

Non-hydrating drinks

Alcohol

Alcohol does not contribute to hydration. It can also affect your baby's health so it's best to avoid it completely in pregnancy (see p.61).

lost due to pregnancy complaints and certain conditions. For example, you will need to replace lost fluids if you are vomiting. (If you are frequently sick and find it hard to keep fluids down, talk to your midwife or healthcare provider.) Sweating can also increase in pregnancy, which will mean you need to replenish fluids, and conditions such as gestational diabetes increase your risk of dehydration.

When you drink enough water, you may notice you start to feel less fatigued, and that symptoms such as constipation improve.

How do I know if I'm dehydrated?

Being aware of the signs of dehydration can alert you to take steps to up your fluid intake and to check with your healthcare provider that there are no other concerns. The following signs indicate dehydration.

- **Urine that is dark yellow or strong-smelling**. Ideally, urine should be colourless to pale yellow and without any odour. Passing urine less frequently – fewer than four times a day – also signals dehydration.
- **You feel thirsty**. By the time you feel thirsty you are likely to already be dehydrated.
- **You feel lightheaded**.
- **You have unexplained fatigue**.
- **Your mouth feels dry** and your eyes less lubricated.

How much should I drink?

The recommendation for adults is to drink 1.5 to 2 litres (2¾ to 3½ pints) of water or other healthy fluids a day. With the extra demands on your body in pregnancy, aim to increase this to 2 to 2.5 litres (3½ to 3¾ pints) a day. A mug or glass is about 250ml (9fl oz), so this equates to 8–10 drinks a day. If drinking 8–10 cups of fluid a day feels daunting, try sipping water throughout the day to stay hydrated.

The diagram opposite looks at the optimal sources of hydration. While plain water is the most hydrating fluid, other drinks can contribute to your fluid intake. Foods with a high water content, such as cucumbers, melons, celery, and tomatoes can also help to refresh the body.

Eating for your baby in pregnancy

Research into brain health and early child development shows resoundingly that the nutrition your baby receives in their first 1,000 days – from conception up to their second birthday – is a key factor, together with their environment and relationships, in shaping their future health through childhood and well beyond.

How pregnancy helps shape your baby's health

Several factors in pregnancy may play a part in your baby's health. The rate you gain weight, your physical and mental wellbeing, and your diet, lifestyle, and environment can all influence how your baby's immune system, metabolism, organ functioning, and bone health develop, and can increase or lower the chance of premature labour or a low birth weight. This impact may reach into adulthood, with growing research suggesting that diabetes, hypertension, and strokes may have origins dating back to pregnancy.

Feeding your baby's brain

Conception through to the first two years of life is the most formative period in your baby's brain development, when the brain grows faster than at any other time. Research suggests that by week 4 of pregnancy, the brain has 10,000 cells and by week 24, 10 billion cells.

Nutrients such as folic acid – crucial for brain health – zinc, iodine, iron, and essential fatty acids, fuel this incredible growth. Pages 48–59 detail the foods and supplements you need for these nutrients. If any of these nutrients is missing from the pregnancy diet, babies are at a greater risk of developmental delays and their cognitive abilities may be affected. Symptoms such as nausea can make it hard to eat a varied diet in pregnancy; in this case, your baby will use the stores you obtained before pregnancy, so a healthy diet when planning a pregnancy is equally important, while pregnancy supplements can make up shortfalls.

Forming tastes in the womb

The foods you eat in pregnancy can also influence your baby's future taste preferences, which in turn can impact their health. Studies suggest that babies can taste a variety of flavours via the amniotic fluid – the liquid that surrounds and cushions them and which they swallow. This fluid has many taste compounds, including sugars such as glucose and fructose, fatty acids, proteins, and salts. Research suggests that babies are born hard-wired to prefer sweet tastes – which signal vital calories and means they do not reject breast milk – and to dislike bitter tastes. However, studies also show that foods such as garlic or carrots, if eaten regularly, can be detected as early as 21 weeks in the womb and that this influence can be continued when breastfeeding, setting a preference for future taste.

Eating junk food occasionally is unlikely to impact your baby's health, and babies' preferences for sweet foods is partly natural, but it makes sense to eat a varied diet when pregnant and breastfeeding (avoiding foods that may be unsafe, see p.60) to enhance the likelihood your baby embraces a variety of foods later on. If nausea makes a varied diet difficult, rest assured that you can also influence your baby's taste when weaning.

Should you avoid allergenic foods in pregnancy?

Some of the most common childhood food allergies are to eggs, milk, peanuts, fish, and shellfish. In the past, pregnant women were advised not to consume peanuts, one of the most potentially severe allergens, to avoid triggering an allergy in their baby, but research has shown that these are safe to eat, and in fact societies who consume more peanuts have fewer nut allergies. Also, there is no evidence that avoiding milk, egg or other potential allergens in pregnancy reduces your child's risk of eczema or asthma. However, restricting your diet may impact your, and in turn your baby's, health as you could become deficient in certain nutrients.

Some research has looked at whether taking a probiotic or an omega-3 supplement in pregnancy could reduce the chance of babies developing a food allergy, but results for both are inconclusive.

Importantly, if you have a food allergy, it doesn't follow that your baby will, too, but there can be a genetic tendency to allergies. If you're concerned, talk to a registered dietitian or nutritionist to discuss your pregnancy diet.

How much should I eat?

Your energy needs for pregnancy and post-birth

The estimated energy needs per day for adult women is around 2,000 calories, but of course everyone has unique requirements so use this as a rough guide. In pregnancy, allowing for individual needs, your energy needs generally rise slightly in the third trimester and you're likely to need extra calories while breastfeeding.

There is a great deal of confusion as to how much women should eat in pregnancy, with many believing popular myths such as "eating for two". In 2017, a survey of 2,100 women found that two-thirds did not know how many extra calories they needed in pregnancy. Of the 140 women in the survey who were pregnant, again almost two-thirds thought they should eat more in the first two trimesters. However, research suggests that putting on excess weight in pregnancy can sometimes increase the risk of poor health for both mum and baby.

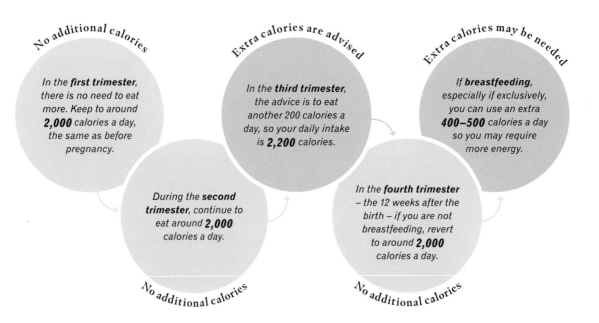

No additional calories

In the **first trimester**, there is no need to eat more. Keep to around **2,000** calories a day, the same as before pregnancy.

During the **second trimester**, continue to eat around **2,000** calories a day.

No additional calories

Extra calories are advised

In the **third trimester**, the advice is to eat another 200 calories a day, so your daily intake is **2,200** calories.

In the **fourth trimester** – the 12 weeks after the birth – if you are not breastfeeding, revert to around **2,000** calories a day.

No additional calories

Extra calories may be needed

If **breastfeeding**, especially if exclusively, you can use an extra **400–500** calories a day so you may require more energy.

Calculating your energy needs

Your body works harder in pregnancy as your blood volume and breathing rate increase to meet the needs of your growing baby. As pregnancy progresses, you'll require more energy as the demands on your body grow, and by the third trimester the recommendation is to have around 200 extra calories a day (see opposite), which could be a cheese sandwich, yogurt and a piece of fruit, a couple of oatcakes with hummus, or two biscuits. If you're breastfeeding, this can use an extra 400–500 calories a day so you may need additional fuel. Bear in mind there's no one-size-fits-all advice for nutrition. The amount of energy you need to consume depends on numerous factors such as your age, genetics, and levels of physical activity.

An awareness of the number of calories you consume is important, but calorie counting isn't always accurate. Being aware of how the type of food you eat converts to energy in the body will help you think about how to maintain a healthy calorie intake. For example, a homemade, wholemeal cheese sandwich is likely to have fewer calories than a highly processed shop-bought one. Processed foods are often more refined, which can cause them to be digested more quickly.

Resisting overeating

In pregnancy, emotions are heightened massively largely due to hormonal shifts. Being aware of using food as a soothing tool or coping strategy now is important as this can lead to unnecessary weight gain that may become long term, affecting overall mental and physical health, and your relationship with food may shift considerably. In pregnancy, excessive weight gain is one of the factors that can increase the risk of conditions such as gestational diabetes (see p.11). The high blood sugar levels that accompany gestational diabetes mean that women need to take extra care of themselves by eating well and keeping active.

Practising "mindful" eating – being fully aware of your emotions, thoughts, and how your body feels as you eat – can help to manage eating. Pay attention to the colours, shapes, aromas, textures, and sounds of food. Focusing on the senses when eating can help to reduce "mindless" eating, reducing the likelihood of weight gain, and in turn reducing pregnancy discomfort. If you're struggling, do reach out to a health professional qualified in ante- and postnatal nutrition or a psychologist.

Your key nutrients

Protein, carbohydrates, and healthy fats – macronutrients – are the key components of our diets, providing the energy we need. A balance of these in pregnancy will ensure your body can cope with the extra demands now and will nourish you and your baby.

Eat enough protein

Protein, made up of amino acids, builds and repairs cells and is key for your baby's growth. In pregnancy, aim to increase your intake slightly, from around 45g (1½oz) to around 70g (2¼oz) a day, including sources with each meal. Proteins are either complete, with all the essential amino acids, or incomplete, with some essential amino acids. Complete proteins are found in meat, poultry, fish, eggs, dairy, and some plant foods such as soya. Limit red meat and choose lean cuts and low-fat dairy to reduce saturated fats. Incomplete proteins are found in plant-based sources such as lentils, beans, peas, chickpeas, nuts, and seeds. Eating a variety of plant proteins over the day, meeting your calorie requirements, will ensure you get all the essential amino acids.

Eat fuelling carbohydrates

Carbs are simple or complex. Simple carbs, found in foods such as pasta and white bread, break down quickly, causing energy spikes and dips. If you're nauseous, though, these blander foods may be easier to face and supply some key nutrients. Pair them with healthy fats and proteins such as nut butter or avocado and seeds to slow the release of energy. Complex carbs contain fibre and starch. Fibre is a key part of our diets. Along with drinking lots of water, it helps regulate digestion and avoid constipation (see p.35). Eat wholegrains, pulses, nuts, seeds, and fibrous veg, such as beetroot, broccoli, and mushrooms.

Pulses and beans supply both protein and fibre, key components of a healthy pregnancy diet.

Oily fish such as salmon are a top source of omega-3s, to support your baby's brain health.

Include healthy fats

Some fat is vital to provide energy, help us absorb fat-soluble vitamins A, D, E, and K, and to ensure we feel full. There are several types of fat: polyunsaturated (omega-3 and -6 essential fatty acids); monounsaturated, and saturated. Trans fats, found in processed food, should be avoided.

Omega-3 essential fatty acids

These essential fatty acids cannot be made by the body so we need to include them in our diets. They come in several forms: docosahexaenoic acid (DHA), alpha-lipoic acid (ALA), and eicosapentaenoic acid (EPA). Omega-3 DHA and EPA are found in oily fish such as salmon and sardines, as well as eggs and fortified dairy. ALA is found in plant-based sources such as soya and nuts and seeds. Omega-3s support heart and brain health, and in pregnancy are important for your baby's brain development. Studies have suggested that pregnant women with a good omega-3 status may have a ten-fold reduced risk of premature labour, but more research is needed to confirm this. As well as benefits in pregnancy, omega-3s are helpful when preparing for pregnancy and after the birth. DHA in particular is thought to promote egg quality and its anti-inflammatory properties promote female fertility. Post-birth, a high concentration in breast milk is thought to help babies' brain and vision development. DHA is also thought to enhance mental focus and may reduce the risk of postnatal depression.

Omega-6 fatty acids, found in vegetable oils and nuts and seeds, also support fetal growth and development. However, too much omega-6 may be harmful to health and we need more omega-3. Western diets tend to favour omega-6, so it's important to eat good omega-3 sources regularly.

Monounsaturated and saturated fats

Monounsaturated fats, found in olives, avocados, and nuts, including nut oils and butters, support the heart, which works hard in pregnancy, and may help reduce blood cholesterol levels. One study also suggested that in pregnancy this fat may help to promote sound sleep.

Saturated fats, found in meat and dairy, like other fats provide energy and help us absorb fat-soluble vitamins. However, they are linked to heart disease, and high amounts in pregnancy to complications such as pre-eclampsia and gestational diabetes, so it is best to limit your intake.

Essential micronutrients

Essential vitamins and minerals and phytonutrients are key for a healthy pregnancy, providing antioxidants and supporting key functions to help optimize your and your baby's health.

Get enough iron

Iron, a vital mineral, facilitates the production of oxygen-carrying haemaglobin in red blood cells. If levels are too low, we feel fatigued, and, in severe cases, can develop iron-deficiency anaemia, increasing the risk of infection and illness. Research suggests that low iron levels can make it harder to conceive and may cause problems such as missed ovulation. In pregnancy, your iron needs increase substantially – almost doubling from 14.8mg to around 27mg a day by the third trimester (more if you develop anaemia) – so you can produce more blood for your growing baby. An inadequate iron intake increases the risk of a low birth weight and may mean your baby is deficient in iron. You also need to replenish iron lost in childbirth. If you're breastfeeding, your iron stores supply your newborn with iron for their development and thyroid function. The good news is that you can obtain sufficient iron by consuming a varied and balanced diet. If supplementation is still needed, your healthcare provider can advise and monitor you. There are two types of iron:

- **Haem iron**, which is more readily absorbed in the body, is found in animal-based sources such as red meat, liver (not recommended during pregnancy due to its high vitamin A content, see p.60), seafood, and eggs.
- **Non-haem iron**, which is less easily absorbed, is found in plant sources such as dark leafy greens, beans, chickpeas, seeds, nuts, tofu, dried fruit, and fortified foods such as cereals and breads. Eat non-haem sources with vitamin C to increase its absorption. For example, finish a meal with citrus fruit or a glass of orange juice, or add vitamin C-rich tomatoes to a bean stew. Avoid drinking tea and coffee for 30 to 60 minutes after consuming iron and vitamin C as caffeine may affect their absorption.

Meet your calcium needs

Your body's demand for calcium is greater in pregnancy and when breastfeeding as you need to ensure you are getting enough to maintain your own bone health, as well as build your baby's bones. Research also suggests that a lack of calcium can increase the risk of developing the condition pre-eclampsia, which leads to high blood pressure and needs careful monitoring. In pregnancy, calcium requirements increase to 1,000mg a day from 700mg a day, and when breastfeeding, to 1,250mg a day.

Good sources of calcium include dairy products such as milk, yogurt, and cheese (reduced-fat may be preferable and choose low-sugar dairy); dark green, leafy vegetables, such as broccoli, collard greens, and bok choy; canned sardines and salmon with bones; calcium-set tofu; almonds; corn tortillas; and fortified orange juice, cereals, and breads. Aim to eat at least three calcium-rich sources throughout the day. Easy ways to add calcium to your diet include enjoying a milk- or yogurt-based smoothie, adding cheese to salads and other dishes, or enjoying a quick snack such as sardines on toast.

Include folate

Folate (vitamin B9) is the natural form of folic acid, which is needed in supplement form in pregnancy (see p.58). Folate plays an important part in the development of healthy red blood cells and the body's nervous system and is also important for the development of our DNA. When planning a pregnancy and in early pregnancy, folate, together with its synthetic form folic acid, is important for egg quality and to prevent neural tube defects in babies. The neural tube forms the early part of the brain and spine within the first 12 weeks of pregnancy and problems in these preliminary stages of development can result in spinal conditions such as spina bifida.

Sources of folate include dark green leafy vegetables such as broccoli, kale, and spinach; a variety of legumes including chickpeas and lentils; asparagus; egg yolks; and poultry. Folic acid is added to some wholemeal and non-gluten breads and some cereals. There are also plans to add it to white bread in the near future.

Eggs are an all-round food for pregnancy, *with many of the nutrients concentrated in the yolk.*

Include sources of zinc

Pre-conception, zinc plays a role in the formation of healthy eggs. It is also important for cell division and protein synthesis. More is needed in pregnancy and when breastfeeding to support your baby's development. Zinc is found in beef, chicken, fish, oysters, eggs, milk, and cheese, and in plant-based sources such as lentils, peas, and beans. Our diets often lack zinc so a supplement may be needed in pregnancy (see p.59).

Think about choline

Choline is thought to work closely with folate at the start of pregnancy to support your baby's brain and neural tube development. Your need of this key nutrient increases in pregnancy and when breastfeeding. The best food sources of choline are eggs and organ meats such as liver, however liver should be avoided in pregnancy because of the high levels of vitamin A (see p.60). It is also found in poultry, cruciferous vegetables, nuts and peanuts, legumes, milk, and soya products. If you are vegan or vegetarian or eat a mainly plant-based diet, it is important to ensure that you are getting enough choline and you may need to speak to your healthcare provider about supplements (see p.59).

Increase your iodine intake

Iodine is used by the thyroid gland to help produce vital growth hormones. It helps to regulate our metabolism and is essential for the healthy development of your baby's brain during pregnancy. Iodine is found mostly in fish and dairy, however, even with dietary sources our levels are often low. If your levels are low when breastfeeding, this could mean your newborn is not getting sufficient iodine and you may need a supplement (see p.59). You may also need to supplement if you are vegan.

Other key minerals

Selenium is important in pregnancy for the normal functioning of the body's cells and immune system. Good sources of selenium include nuts such as Brazil nuts and seafood. Other important nutrients to include in your diet during pregnancy include potassium, magnesium, manganese, copper, and chromium. Including a variety of fresh produce and pulses in your diet should provide sufficient amounts of these nutrients.

Fat-soluble vitamins A, D, and E

Vitamins A, D, and E need to be eaten with fat to be absorbed. Vitamin A supports the development of your baby's vision and organs, though high levels, found in liver and some supplements (check omega-3 supplements and avoid cod liver oil), should be avoided in pregnancy as they can cause birth defects (see p.60). Safe levels are found in dairy, eggs, and oily fish. Beta-carotene, found in spinach and bright produce such as peppers, sweet potatoes, and apricots, converts to vitamin A in the body.

Vitamin D, found in fatty fish such as salmon, fortified dairy and orange juice, and egg yolks, works with calcium to help your baby's bones and teeth develop. It also supports hormone and immune system function and brain health and may reduce the risk of postnatal depression. It can be hard to get enough from your diet, so supplements are key (see p.58). Vitamin E, found in plant oils, nuts, seeds, avocado, spinach, and eggs, may aid fertility and adequate levels may reduce the risk of pre-eclampsia and early labour.

B vitamins and vitamin C

The family of B vitamins, found in meat, poultry, seafood, eggs, beans, and fortified foods, plays a key role in energy production and your baby's development. B12 in particular supports fertility, with a lack of B12 linked to problems with ovulation. It is also involved in folate metabolism so is important in pregnancy. Research suggests that babies with low levels may be more irritable. B12 is found in beef, salmon, clams, tuna, eggs, and dairy. If you are following a vegetarian or vegan diet, you will need to supplement and/or eat fortified dairy alternatives and cereals.

Vitamin C helps support blood vessels and bones. In pregnancy, it is thought that maintaining levels of vitamin C also supports the placenta. Sources include oranges, orange juice, red and green peppers, strawberries, blackcurrants, broccoli, Brussels sprouts, and potatoes.

Phytonutrients

Research shows that the antioxidant plant nutrients, carotenoids, which include lycopene and beta-carotene, may help to reduce the risk of pre-eclampsia, support your baby's growth, and play a role in reducing the chances of premature labour. Sources include carrots, papaya, sweet potatoes, tomatoes, squash, broccoli, and leafy greens.

Summer berries *have a range of protective antioxidants and essential vitamins.*

Pregnancy supplements

Optimizing nutrition before even planning for a baby is wise as deficits can impact fertility, pregnancy, and any future baby's health. Ideally, your diet meets your nutritional needs, but studies show that most women of reproductive age are low in folate, iodine, and iron. If you are planning to conceive, start taking an antenatal supplement 3–6 months before pregnancy and supplement in pregnancy as needed. The chart here looks at the key pregnancy nutrients that may need supplementing. Types and dosage vary based on your needs, so consult a registered nutritionist.

Folic acid

Folic acid is the synthetic form of folate (see p.53). Taking folic acid supplements before conception and during pregnancy reduces the risk of neural tube defects, such as spina bifida, in the baby. The neural tube forms the early part of the brain and spinal cord during the first trimester, so it begins to form often before women know they are pregnant.

Supplementing *Women are advised to take folic acid supplements of 400mcg a day before conception and up until the 12th week of pregnancy. In some cases, folic acid requirements are above 400mcg, for example, if there is a family history of neural tube problems, so check the amount in your supplement and talk to your healthcare provider.*

Vitamin D

We get this mainly from synthesizing sunlight so it can be low in winter. It has a role in hormone and immune system function, cell division, and bone health in baby and mum.

Supplementing *This can be ergocalciferol (vegetable-based) or cholecalciferol (animal-based). If you take a multi-vitamin supplement with at least 10mcg vitamin D this will meet your needs (unless advised by a health professional that you need more).*

Calcium

This is key for your own and your baby's bone health (see p.53).

Supplementing *You need 1,000mg daily in pregnancy (up from 700mg) and 1,250mg daily when breastfeeding so supplement dietary sources if needed.*

Vitamin B12

This aids egg formation, ovulation, and folate metabolism in the body and nervous system so is important in pregnancy.

Supplementing *Look for cobalamin, or, ideally, the activated form, methylcobalamin. It's especially important to supplement in pregnancy if vegan as plant foods are low in this vitamin.*

Iron

Your needs almost double from 14.8mg to 27mg daily in pregnancy, to produce more blood to support your baby's growth.

Supplementing *This may be needed if you are anaemic but constipation is a side-effect so your healthcare provider can advise. Iron absorption can be inhibited by other nutrients in supplements so it can be best to take iron at a different time of the day.*

Omega-3 essential fatty acids

These are important (especially DHA) in optimizing egg quality. Pregnant women with a good omega-3 status may reduce the risk of early labour ten-fold.

Supplementing *You need at least 300mg of DHA a day. If your antenatal or pregnancy supplement does not provide this, you can take a separate algae-based omega-3 supplement in addition to dietary sources (see p.51) to be on the safe side.*

Zinc

Plays a key role in healthy egg formation, cell division, and your baby's growth.

Supplementing *Look for around 11mg of zinc in an antenatal (and pregnancy) supplement as well as ensuring that your diet contains sources (see p.55).*

Iodine

This is often low, especially in plant-based diets. It has a key role in thyroid health. Low levels can impact your baby's growth in pregnancy and when breastfeeding.

Supplementing *Pregnancy and breastfeeding supplements should contain 200–290mcg respectively. If you have a history of thyroid concerns, talk to your healthcare provider before supplementing.*

Choline

This is key for brain and neural tube development, working closely with the nutrient folate at the start of pregnancy.

Supplementing *Non-vegetarian diets tend to have plenty of choline (see p.55). If your diet is plant-based, it's important to ensure you're getting enough choline so talk to your healthcare provider about supplements.*

Other nutrients

A few other key nutrients to look out for in an antenatal and pregnancy supplement are niacin (vitamin B3), selenium, magnesium, and vitamin K.

Which foods should I avoid in pregnancy?

Certain foods pose a direct risk to your baby in pregnancy and others can affect your own health, which in turn may impact your baby. Being aware of what to avoid in pregnancy and practising food hygiene is important to keep you and your baby safe.

What are the guidelines?

In the UK, the advice is that some foods either should be avoided, limited, or eaten with caution in pregnancy. Generally, ensure food is chilled as required, that cooked or reheated food is eaten while hot, and that food is not kept beyond its "use by" date.

- **Meat should be cooked through**, with no pinkness or blood. Parasites can live inside raw meat and cause the condition toxoplasmosis, which increases the risks of miscarriage and, very occasionally, can cause birth defects. Take extra care when cooking items such as sausages, mince, and burgers. Also, avoid game meats such as goose, partridge, or pheasant, as they may contain lead shot.

- **Liver and liver products such as pâté** should not be eaten. Liver is naturally high in vitamin A, which in excess can be harmful to your baby. (You should also avoid multivitamins or cod liver oil with vitamin A.)

- **All pâtés** should be avoided, including vegetable ones, as they can contain listeria, a bacteria that may lead to listeriosis, which can cause miscarriage, stillbirth, premature labour, and serious illness in newborns.

- **Some cheeses** should be avoided to limit the risk of listeria infection. The diagram, right, lists which are safe in pregnancy, and those that should be avoided or heated through to kill off any bacteria.

- **Some raw and undercooked eggs** should be avoided. In the UK, eggs with a British red lion stamp are at a very low risk for salmonella so are safe to eat in pregnancy, both runny and raw. Eggs without this stamp should be well cooked before consuming in pregnancy.

Safe in pregnancy

Hard/firm cheeses, both pasteurized and unpasteurized

- Cheddar
- Parmesan
- Stilton (stick to pasteurized)

Soft, processed pasteurized cheeses

- mozzarella
- paneer
- feta
- goat's cheese without the rind
- cottage cheese
- cream cheese
- halloumi
- ricotta

Avoid in pregnancy

The following cheeses may harbour listeria so should be avoided:

- soft blue-veined cheeses such as Danish blue, Gorgonzola, Roquefort, and dolcelatte
- soft mould-ripened cheeses such as Brie, Camembert, and rinded goat's cheese

Safe in pregnancy when heated

If heated through thoroughly, soft blue-veined cheeses and soft mould-ripened cheeses (see above) are safe to eat in pregnancy.

Which cheeses are safe to eat?

Hard cheeses (pasteurized and unpasteurized) and processed soft cheeses are safe in pregnancy; other cheeses are safe only if heated thoroughly.

- **Salads** should be washed thoroughly before eating and any that have been left out of the fridge for a while should be avoided.
- **Avoid shark**, swordfish, and marlin. These have high levels of mercury, which can affect your baby's nervous system. Tuna also has mercury so limit it to no more than four cans or two steaks a week. Limit all oily fish to two portions a week as they contain pollutants. Likewise, limit sea bass, sea bream, halibut, crab, turbot, and dogfish. There are no limits on shellfish but ensure it's cooked. Sushi is safe if fish has been frozen and it is from a reputable place. Avoid sushi that has sat out of the fridge. Smoked salmon sushi does not need freezing first as it has been cured.
- **Caffeine**, found in drinks, chocolate, and medications, should be limited to no more than 200mg a day (see p.42). Research links over-consumption to low birth weight and pregnancy complications.
- **Alcohol** should be avoided. Fetal alcohol syndrome (FAS) can severely impact development and the advice is that no amount of alcohol is safe.
- **Allergenic foods** are safe unless, of course, you have a specific allergy.

Your pregnancy lifestyle

As well as diet, your daily lifestyle impacts your pregnancy. Whether you sit for long periods of time at a desk or on a commute or walk and move around a lot, and the quality of sleep you enjoy, all affect your wellbeing. There is no one perfect lifestyle, but by trying to stay active and, ideally, building in exercise time and prioritizing sleep and rest, you will be equipped to deal with daily stressors and will support the health of your growing baby.

Staying active in pregnancy

Listening to your body is key, resting when you feel tired, but ultimately it's incredibly important to move around in pregnancy as much as you can. Understanding how to stay active and exercise safely in pregnancy will help you to take the best possible care of your body as it undergoes the many changes that take place throughout these nine months.

Strength and fitness

Being strong in pregnancy helps your joints to withstand the extra pressure caused by your growing baby so that you can get on with everyday activities as far as possible. As your baby grows and your bump moves outwards, your pelvis develops an anterior tilt, changing your posture slightly. By keeping your muscles strong and activated, you will help to ensure that these slight postural changes don't cause unwanted aches and pains.

Strength training can sound offputting, but exercises such as Pilates, yoga, gentle weightlifting, bodyweight exercises such as lunges and squats, walking, swimming, and cycling are all forms of strength training.

Your cardiovascular fitness is also key in pregnancy. Carrying around the extra weight from your growing baby can be exhausting, so maintaining a good level of fitness helps to make this more manageable.

Keeping active and moving around will support a healthy blood flow, key for your health and your baby's development. A good level of cardio fitness can be achieved by walking, cycling, swimming, or simply playing with an older child.

Both strength building and cardio fitness build stamina for labour and birth and support your recovery after the birth. Movement and exercise also release the feel-good hormones, endorphins, into your body, helping you feel positive and energized in pregnancy.

Your pregnancy exercise regime

The type of exercise you choose depends on your own circumstances. If you exercised before pregnancy, you can continue your regime if you feel able to do so. Generally, if you feel good while exercising, there is no reason to stop. Our bodies are more capable than we tend to think in pregnancy, as long as we listen to signs to rest (see below). As your bump grows, you may need to modify exercise such as running and focus on gentler activities such as walking and swimming. The following guidelines will help you to exercise safely in pregnancy.

- **If you are taking up a new form of exercise** in pregnancy, seek advice from a qualified teacher and/or attend a pregnancy class where you will be guided appropriately. Avoid taking up strenuous exercise now; start gently and choose something you think you will enjoy, which you will be likely to stick with.
- **Use the "talk" test**. If you can talk a little during your workout or even have a conversation, then the pace is a sensible one for you. If at any stage you feel so out of breath that you can't talk, take a break to let your heart rate come down, then resume at a slower pace or reduced intensity.
- **If at any point you feel dizzy**, lightheaded, in pain, or are struggling for breath, stop immediately. These signs are your body's way of telling you it isn't coping with the intensity of exercise. If you feel concerned, contact your midwife or doctor before continuing.
- **Avoid lying on your back** for a long time in the second and third trimesters.

When to resume exercising after the birth

It can be tempting to dive straight back in to an exercise regime after the birth, but it is important to take the time needed to recover properly. It is best to wait a minimum of six weeks before resuming exercise. However, when you feel ready to, you can start lengthening your walking distances, stretching, and reintroducing pelvic floor exercises, all of which will help your body to recover.

Sleeping well in pregnancy

Getting sufficient sleep is imperative in pregnancy. Your body burns an incredible amount of energy to support your growing baby, so your sleep needs increase to 8–10 hours sleep a night. However, a range of factors can leave you feeling fatigued and make sleeping through a challenge. In the first trimester, high levels of progesterone can cause sleepiness, while nausea can keep you awake. Later in pregnancy, symptoms such as restless legs, heartburn, and leg cramps, as well as your larger bump, can make it hard to relax. In addition, as your growing bump presses on your bladder, you may need to get up regularly to go to the toilet.

As well as physical obstacles, emotional factors can keep you awake. You may feel anxious about becoming a mother, or, with a subsequent pregnancy, worried about adding to your family. As the birth approaches, you may start to worry increasingly about the delivery.

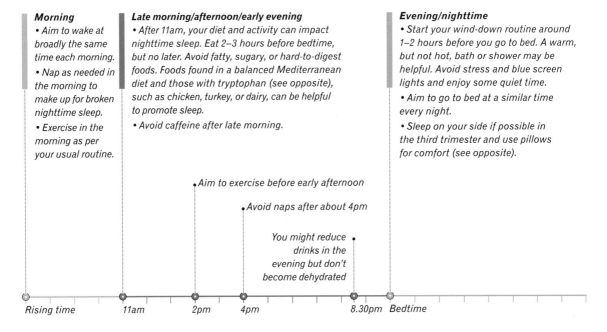

Morning
• Aim to wake at broadly the same time each morning.
• Nap as needed in the morning to make up for broken nighttime sleep.
• Exercise in the morning as per your usual routine.

Late morning/afternoon/early evening
• After 11am, your diet and activity can impact nighttime sleep. Eat 2–3 hours before bedtime, but no later. Avoid fatty, sugary, or hard-to-digest foods. Foods found in a balanced Mediterranean diet and those with tryptophan (see opposite), such as chicken, turkey, or dairy, can be helpful to promote sleep.
• Avoid caffeine after late morning.

Evening/nighttime
• Start your wind-down routine around 1–2 hours before you go to bed. A warm, but not hot, bath or shower may be helpful. Avoid stress and blue screen lights and enjoy some quiet time.
• Aim to go to bed at a similar time every night.
• Sleep on your side if possible in the third trimester and use pillows for comfort (see opposite).

• Aim to exercise before early afternoon

• Avoid naps after about 4pm

You might reduce drinks in the evening but don't become dehydrated •

Rising time   11am   2pm   4pm   8.30pm   Bedtime

A sleep guide for pregnancy
Daily life can make it hard to stick to routines consistently, so use this timeline as a rough guide to help you enjoy a good night's sleep.

If you are struggling to sleep at night, try to supplement your sleep with daytime naps when possible. If you don't have other children to care for, try to nap at weekends and get earlier nights. Practise good sleep hygiene, too. The daily timeline opposite sets out the ideal times to nap, exercise, eat, and drink, and suggests how to wind down before bed.

The best position for sleep

As pregnancy progresses, finding a comfortable sleeping position can be hard. It's also thought that sleeping positions can impact the baby's health. Research shows that sleeping on your side (ideally your left but either side is fine) is safest for your baby in the third trimester, as lying on your back can place pressure on the main vein that carries blood to the heart, increasing the risk of stillbirth. Rest assured that if your pregnancy is uncomplicated, your risk of stillbirth is relatively low (1 in 200). Going to sleep on your side reduces this risk further. If you awake lying on your back, simply turn to your side. A supportive pillow between your knees and, later on, to support your bump can be helpful.

The relationship between nutrition and sleep

Research has found that people who sleep for less time often eat foods with a higher fat content. In pregnancy, your aim is to eat a balanced, Mediterranean-style diet (see p.13). The Mediterranean lifestyle has been associated with better sleep hygiene and a lower risk of insomnia, so this can support sleep now. Eating foods such as poultry and dairy that contain the amino acid tryptophhan, the precursor to the sleep hormones melatonin and serotonin, may also promote healthy sleep. Be mindful of the following foods and drinks, which can hamper sleep.

- **Caffeine**, found in coffee, tea, chocolate, and energy and fizzy drinks, is a stimulant that can be helpful earlier in the day, but later on can affect sleep. It can also impact your baby's health in pregnancy, so you should avoid it or limit to no more than 200mg a day (see p.61).
- **Hard-to-digest foods** such as ultra-processed meats and deep-fried foods can keep you awake at night as your body tries to process them.
- **Drinking alcohol** before bedtime can cause you to wake repeatedly. The advice in pregnancy is to avoid alcohol altogether (see p.61).

Recipes
for pregnancy

This selection of more than 80 delicious and easy-to-make recipes provides inspiration for meals throughout pregnancy. Pages 68–69 offer tailored suggestions for the best recipes to suit fluctuating appetites and energy levels in pregnancy, and all the recipes deliver key nutrients to nourish you and your baby.

Tailoring meals for pregnancy trimesters

All the recipes in this book can be enjoyed throughout your pregnancy. However, how you feel at different times in pregnancy can affect your appetite. This trimester recipe plan suggests ways to tailor meals as symptoms cause your appetite to dip or grow. All oven temperatures are for fan ovens; add 20°C for non-fan ovens.

Helpful recipes: first trimester

Nausea and fatigue in trimester one can mean you favour unfussy meals. The following simple, but nutritious, recipes can work well now.

Helpful recipes: second trimester

You may feel re-energized and find a healthy appetite returns in this trimester. This is the time to eat a wide variety of colourful foods to maximize your nutrient intake.

Helpful recipes: third trimester

As your bump grows and fatigue, and sometimes nausea, return, light bites and simple meals may be the most desirable.

Helpful recipes: fourth trimester

Exhaustion can set in but nutrient demands are high. These easy to make, fuelling recipes are ideal now.

Breakfasts

Our first meal of the day is often given little thought, with the same breakfast bowl repeated over the week. The recipes here treat breakfast as an opportunity to refuel for the day ahead and add a variety of essential nutrients to your pregnancy diet.

The following breakfasts include quick-to-prep options – perfect for rushed mornings, which is often the case if you already have young children to look after – and more leisurely recipes for weekends and holidays. Sometimes you may feel you need to eat something simple as soon as you wake to quell pregnancy-related nausea; in this case, keep an oat cake or a handful of nuts by your bedside.

The delicious sweet and savoury recipes cater for all pregnancy appetites. Simple but nutritious recipes for oats, pancakes, and eggy toast are perfect when queasiness saps your appetite. When nausea recedes, easy-to-add toppings and variations with fruits, greens, nuts, and seeds help you maximize your nutrient intake. Chocolate porridge and fruity toppings can help to satisfy sweet cravings, while greens-based dishes encourage you to broaden your breakfast repertoire. When your appetite is strong, breakfast and brunch wraps, frittata, and fritters offer a satisfying start to the day – or meal at any time. Dotted throughout, flex ideas offer easy swaps for particular dietary requirements. Each recipe provides a delicious and nutritious breakfast plate to keep you going throughout the morning.

Banana, almond, *and* ginger pancakes

Serves 2
Prep 10 mins
Cook 10 mins

125g (4¹/₂oz) porridge oats
125g (4¹/₂oz) plain flour
25g (scant 1oz) ground
   almonds
2 tsp baking powder
2 tsp ground ginger
pinch of salt
1 overripe banana,
   mashed
1¹/₂ tbsp rapeseed oil
1 tbsp maple syrup
250ml (9fl oz)
   semi-skimmed milk or
   fortified plant-based
   alternative
1 tbsp coconut oil
extra banana slices and
   maple syrup, to serve

supports heart health • provides sustained energy • promotes healthy digestion

Simple and nutritious, these tasty pancakes deliver fibre and healthy fats from the oats, bananas, and almonds, providing slow release energy and supporting digestion and the heart, both of which work extra hard in pregnancy.

Preheat the oven to 50°C (122°F/Gas ¼). Place the oats in a food processor and blitz into a flour. Combine the oat flour, plain flour, almonds, baking powder, ginger, and salt in a bowl. Add the banana, rapeseed oil, maple syrup, and milk, then whisk to form a smooth batter. The batter should drop off a spoon – if it is a little thick, add a dash more milk and whisk again.

Heat the coconut oil in a frying pan over a medium heat. Spoon circles of the batter – about 2 tablespoons each – into the pan in batches of two or three at a time. Cook for 2–3 minutes, until the edges set and the surface bubbles. Flip the pancakes and cook for another 2–3 minutes, until the base is golden. Keep warm in the oven while you repeat with the remaining batter. Stack the pancakes between 2 plates and top with banana slices and a drizzle of maple syrup.

Banana, almond, and ginger pancakes

Peach, ricotta, *and* pistachio toast

Serves 2
Prep 5 mins
Cook 30 mins

3 ripe peaches, halved and pitted
2 tbsp olive oil
2 tbsp honey or maple syrup, plus extra to drizzle (optional)
1 tsp brown sugar
1 tsp ground cinnamon
2 large slices of sourdough
5 tbsp ricotta cheese
chopped toasted pistachios, to serve

supports bone health • supports immune system function • provides key micronutrients

Follow the classic tradition of pairing cheese and fruit with a delicious ricotta and peach combo, adding vitamin C and calcium to your toast. Most soft cheeses need heating through in pregnancy, but as a pasteurized cheese, ricotta is safe to eat cold.

Preheat the oven to 160°C (350°F/Gas 4). Place the peach halves in an ovenproof dish, cut-side up. Put the olive oil, honey or maple syrup, sugar, and cinnamon in a small bowl and stir to combine. Spoon the mixture over the peaches and bake for 30 minutes, or until the peaches are easily pierced with a fork and starting to caramelize.

Toast the sourdough as preferred. Spread the toast with the ricotta and arrange the roasted peach halves on top. Sprinkle over the pistachios and, if desired, drizzle over a little extra honey or maple syrup to serve.

Flex it – *For a vegan breakfast, replace the ricotta with a dairy-free cream cheese, and opt for the maple syrup instead of the honey.*

Savoury spinach pancakes

Serves 2
Prep 10 mins
Cook 15 mins

150g (5½oz) spinach
175g (6oz) wholemeal flour
1 tsp baking powder
pinch of salt
1 egg
200ml (7fl oz) semi-skimmed
   milk or fortified plant-based
   alternative
1 tbsp olive oil
200g (7oz) mushrooms, sliced
4 tbsp cream cheese
50g (1¾oz) smoked salmon
   (optional)

provides sustained energy • provides antioxidants

Hard to resist, simple pancakes are perfect when nausea takes hold, ensuring you get some protein and fuelling carbs. Adding antioxidant-rich spinach makes a nutrient-dense breakfast, brunch, or main.

Preheat the oven to 50°C (122°F/Gas ¼). Place the spinach in a large bowl and pour boiling water over. Leave to soak for 2 minutes, then drain, transfer to a blender, and pulse to a purée. Combine the spinach purée, flour, baking powder, and a pinch of salt in a bowl. Add the egg and milk and whisk to form a smooth batter.

Heat a little of the oil in a non-stick frying pan over a medium heat. Once hot, spoon a ladleful (about 2 tablespoons) of batter into the pan to form a small circle. Do this in batches of two or three pancakes at a time. Cook for 2–3 minutes, until the edges are set and bubbles appear on the surface. Flip the pancakes and cook for a further 2–3 minutes, until golden. Keep warm in the oven while you repeat with the remaining batter.

In the meantime, heat another frying pan over a medium heat and add the remaining oil. Add the mushrooms and fry, stirring frequently, for 6–8 minutes, or until browned and softened. Enjoy the warm pancakes with a layer of cream cheese between them, topped with the mushrooms and, if using, smoked salmon.

Breakfast wrap

Makes 1
Prep 5 mins
Cook 10 mins

1 tbsp olive oil
4 cherry tomatoes,
    quartered
1 garlic clove, crushed
2 large eggs
salt and freshly ground
    black pepper
20g (¾oz) Cheddar, grated
2 tbsp refried black beans
1 tbsp coriander, leaves and
    stems, chopped
1 wholemeal wrap
¼ avocado, pitted and sliced

**promotes healthy digestion • provides
key micronutrients**

Ideal for breakfast or lunch, this wrap is packed with
nutrients. Eggs supply iron, iodine, and vitamins B12
and D, all key in pregnancy. Paired with avocado for
healthy fats, hydrating tomatoes, and protein-providing
black beans, this creates a go-to balanced meal.

Heat the oil in a frying pan (about the size of the wrap)
over a medium heat. Once hot, add the tomatoes and
garlic and fry for 2–3 minutes, until the tomatoes are soft.

Beat the eggs in a small bowl with a pinch of salt and
pepper. Increase the heat of the pan slightly, then add
the eggs, swirling them around to reach the edges of
the pan. Make sure that the tomatoes are evenly
distributed across the pan.

Working quickly, arrange the Cheddar, refried beans,
and coriander evenly over the eggs, then top with the
wrap. Press the wrap into the omelette, using the still
slightly uncooked egg to glue them together. Cook for
a minute or so, or until the egg has cooked through. Flip
the omelette and the wrap over and cook for a further
minute, or until the base of the wrap is golden brown.
Top with the avocado, then fold the wrap up. Remove
from the pan, chop in half, and enjoy warm.

Avocado *and* feta toast

Serves 2
Prep 5 mins

1 avocado, flesh only
a squeeze of lemon juice, plus
**   lemon wedges, to serve**
salt and freshly ground
**   black pepper**
2 large slices of sourdough,
**   ideally wholemeal**
40g (1½oz) feta cheese
2 tbsp mixed seeds
pinch of smoked paprika

Flex it *– For a vegan dish, replace*
the feta with a non-dairy alternative.

promotes healthy digestion • provides sustained energy

A modern-day classic, this is perfect for those days when nausea or your growing bump mean you want something light but filling and nutritionally balanced. Avocado provides healthy fats, fibre, and vitamin E; feta supplies protein; and delicious sourdough adds carbs.

Use a fork to mash the avocado in a bowl, then add the lemon juice and a pinch of salt and pepper and combine. Taste and add more lemon juice or seasoning as required.

Toast the sourdough slices as desired, then spread with the crushed avocado and crumble over the feta cheese. Sprinkle with the mixed seeds, a pinch of paprika, and a crack of pepper. Serve with lemon wedges on the side.

Avocado and feta toast

Spicy tofu *and* greens brunch

Serves 3–4
Prep 10 mins
Cook 25 mins

3 tbsp olive oil
1 onion, finely diced
2 green peppers, deseeded
   and finely diced
3 garlic cloves, crushed
1 tsp ground cumin
1 tsp smoked paprika
¼ tsp cayenne pepper
salt and freshly ground
   black pepper
200g (7oz) spinach
250g (9oz) frozen peas
225g (8oz) tofu (opt for
   calcium-set tofu for
   extra calcium)
handful of coriander,
   leaves and stems,
   roughly chopped
200ml (7fl oz) single cream
plain yogurt, chilli flakes,
   and warm crusty bread,
   to serve

Flex it – *For a vegan dish, use soya cream in place of cream and opt for dairy-free yogurt.*

supports bone health • plant-based protein source

Full of flavour, this weekend brunch treat is brimming with antioxidant-rich greens, while tofu and yogurt provide protein and calcium, supporting your baby's growth and bone development.

Heat half the oil in a frying pan over a medium heat. Add the onion and peppers and cook for 8–10 minutes. Add the garlic and stir for a minute or so, until soft. Add the cumin, paprika, and cayenne, season, and fry for a minute, or until the spices release their aromas. Add 150ml (5fl oz) of water and bring to the boil. Cook for 3 minutes, adding a splash more water if it begins to dry out.

In the meantime, pulse the spinach in a processor to a paste. Bring a pan of lightly salted water to the boil, add the peas, and cook for 2 minutes. Drain and set aside.

Drain the tofu, then use a clean tea towel to press down on it to remove excess moisture. Slice the tofu into strips and press down on them again with the towel until no moisture is left on the surface. Heat the remaining oil in a separate frying pan. Fry the tofu for 2–3 minutes each side, until golden. Remove from the pan and set aside.

Add the spinach, peas, coriander, and cream to the frying pan. Stir and allow to bubble on a low heat for 5 minutes, until slightly thickened. Top with the tofu and serve with a drizzle of yogurt, some chilli flakes, and warm crusty bread.

Overnight oats three ways

Serves 1
Prep 5 mins

45g (1½oz) porridge oats
100ml (3½fl oz) semi-skimmed
milk or fortified plant-based
alternative
4 tbsp Greek yogurt
1–2 tbsp honey or maple syrup
(optional)

For carrot and raisin oats
1 small carrot, grated
2 tbsp raisins
1 tsp flaxseeds

For vanilla berry oats
1 tsp vanilla extract
To serve:
2 tbsp almond butter, handful
of berries (whichever are
in season), and 1 tbsp
pumpkin seeds

For cocoa and orange oats
1½ tsp cocoa powder
zest of 1 orange
To serve:
1 tbsp cacao nibs

provides sustained energy • promotes healthy digestion • provides antioxidants

A source of fibre and sustained energy, oats, like other wholegrains, also support heart health in pregnancy. Oats pair naturally with a wide range of flavours, making it easy to add antioxidant-rich ingredients to your breakfast bowl.

Place the porridge oats, milk, yogurt, and, if using, honey or maple syrup in a lidded airtight container. Add the pairing option of your choice to the oat mixture, holding back any extra serving ingredients. Mix well and cover with the lid. Refrigerate overnight, or for at least 2 hours, before serving.

For the berry oats, drizzle over the almond butter and serve topped with the berries and pumpkin seeds. For the cocoa oats, serve topped with the cacao nibs.

Eggy toast three ways

Serves 1
Prep 5 mins
Cook 6–10 mins

1 large egg
1 tbsp semi-skimmed milk or
    fortified plant-based
    alternative
2 slices of bread
½ tbsp butter

Banana and cinnamon topping
½ tbsp butter
1 tbsp maple syrup, plus
    a drizzle more, to serve
½ tsp cinnamon, plus an extra
    pinch, to serve
1 banana, sliced
50g (1¾oz) Greek yogurt

Spinach and tomato topping
2 tsp olive oil
1 garlic clove, crushed
60g (2oz) cherry tomatoes
2 large handfuls of spinach
salt and freshly ground
    black pepper
2 tsp grated Parmesan

Avocado and seeds topping
½ avocado, mashed
salt and freshly ground
    black pepper
1 tbsp mixed seeds
pinch of smoked paprika

provides sustained energy • has key nutrients

Simple eggy toast is ideal if nausea hits, delivering vital protein. When your appetite returns, add toppings for extra nutrients and a perfectly balanced meal.

Place the egg and milk in a shallow bowl and beat together. Soak the bread in the egg mix, until all the liquid is absorbed. Heat a frying pan over a medium heat. Add the butter and swirl it around. Once it starts to foam, fry the bread for 2–3 minutes each side, until golden. Transfer to a plate and serve straight away with your chosen topping.

For the banana topping, heat a frying pan over a medium heat. Add the butter, maple syrup, and cinnamon, and stir until the butter starts to bubble. Add the banana slices and fry for 1–2 minutes each side, until golden and caramelized. Serve over the toast with the Greek yogurt, a drizzle of maple syrup, and a pinch more cinnamon.

For the spinach topping, heat the olive oil in a frying pan over a medium heat. Add the garlic and fry for 1 minute. Halve the tomatoes and fry for a further 2 minutes, stirring constantly until the garlic is golden and the tomatoes softened. Add the spinach, season, and stir until the spinach is wilted. Serve over the toast, sprinkled with Parmesan.

For the avocado topping, season the avocado. Serve over the toast, sprinkled with the seeds and paprika.

(photographed overleaf)

Eggy toast three ways

Chocolate porridge

provides sustained energy • provides antioxidants

This deliciously indulgent chocolate porridge is actually full of goodness for you and your baby. Fibre-rich oats release energy slowly and keep digestion moving. Topping with berries – or a fruit of choice – and hazelnuts, adds health-enhancing antioxidants.

Serves 1
Prep 5 mins
Cook 10 mins

45g (1½oz) porridge oats
1 tsp flaxseed
1 tsp cocoa powder
1 tbsp maple syrup (optional)
pinch of salt

250ml (9fl oz) semi-skimmed milk or fortified plant-based alternative
2 squares of dark chocolate, minimum 75 per cent cocoa
handful of berries (whatever is in season)
10g (¼oz) hazelnuts, toasted and roughly chopped

Place the oats, flaxseed, cocoa powder, maple syrup (if using), salt, and milk in a small saucepan over a medium heat and stir to combine. Bring to a simmer, then stir regularly until the porridge reaches the desired consistency.

In the meantime, melt the chocolate in a bain-marie or a bowl in your microwave on the lowest setting, stirring every 20 seconds if using a microwave to prevent it from burning.

Pour the porridge into a bowl and top with the berries, toasted hazelnuts, and melted chocolate. Enjoy straightaway.

Chocolate porridge

Veggie fritters *with* poached eggs *and* avocado

Serves 2
Prep 10 mins
Cook 20 mins

198g can sweetcorn, drained
100g (3½oz) courgette, grated and patted dry
2 spring onions, finely chopped
1 tsp cayenne pepper
1 tsp paprika
3 tbsp self-raising flour
5 eggs – 1 beaten, 4 for poaching (choose red lion stamp for poached eggs in pregnancy
30ml (1fl oz) semi-skimmed milk or fortified plant-based alternative
salt and freshly ground black pepper
drizzle of olive oil
1 avocado
handful of sun-dried tomatoes, sliced
juice of ½ lime, plus lime wedges, to serve
pinch of chipotle chilli flakes

provides sustained energy • supports fetal development

These satisfying fritters serve brunch and lunch. Eggs, avocado, and veg create a perfect balance of protein, fats, and carbs. Eggs also supply hard-to-source choline and iodine, key for fetal brain development.

Place the sweetcorn, courgette, and spring onions in a bowl with the cayenne, paprika, and flour, and mix until the vegetables are well coated with the flour and spices. Add the beaten egg and milk, stir well, and season.

Bring a pan of water to the boil. In the meantime, place a frying pan over a medium heat and heat the oil. Spoon in 6 scoops of the fritter mixture, flattening them into patties. Fry for 3 minutes, or until golden, then flip to cook the other side. For the best results, fry in batches.

While the fritters cook, poach the eggs in two batches. Add a drop of vinegar to the water and stir to make a whirlpool. Gently crack each egg in and simmer on a low heat for 2 minutes. Remove the pan from the heat. Stand the eggs in the water for 30 seconds, then use a slotted spoon to remove them and drain them on a kitchen towel.

Mash the avocado with a fork and combine with the sun-dried tomatoes, lime juice, and chilli flakes. Serve the fritters with the avocado, layering if you wish, the poached eggs on top, and lime wedges on the side.

Greens *and* cheese frittata

Serves 4
Prep 5 mins
Cook 35–40 mins

½ head of broccoli, cut
    into small florets
8 large eggs
100g (3½oz) Cheddar
salt and freshly ground
    black pepper
2 tbsp olive oil
2 garlic cloves, crushed
4 spring onions, finely
    chopped
3 large handfuls of
    spinach

Flex it – *Feel free to throw
in any veggies you have in
the fridge that need using
up, prioritizing dark, leafy
greens to provide folate.*

provides key micronutrients • supports a healthy gut • promotes healthy digestion

Tasty and simple, this frittata keeps protein levels topped up while also supplying key micronutrients such as iodine and choline to support your baby's growing brain. Onions provide prebiotic fibre, promoting gut health through pregnancy.

Preheat the oven to 160°C (350°F/Gas 4). Steam the broccoli florets for 3–4 minutes, or until al dente. In a measuring jug or large bowl, gently beat the eggs together with the Cheddar and a good pinch of salt and pepper. Set aside.

Heat an ovenproof frying pan over a medium heat and add the oil. Once hot, add the garlic and spring onions and fry for 1 minute. Add the spinach and a pinch of seasoning and cook for a further 1–2 minutes, or until the spinach is wilted.

Arrange the broccoli evenly around the pan with the other vegetables, then pour in the egg mixture. Remove the pan from the heat and transfer to the oven to bake for 30–35 minutes, until the frittata has puffed up and is golden on top. Cut into slices and serve warm or cold.

Greens and cheese frittata

Nut butter *and* raspberry toast

Serves 2
Prep 5 mins

4 slices of sourdough,
    or bread of choice
almond butter – enough
    to cover the toast, plus
    extra to drizzle
2 handfuls of raspberries
a handful of pumpkin
    seeds, to serve

Flex it – *Substitute the almond butter with peanut butter if you prefer.*

provides sustained energy • supports heart health • provides key micronutrients

Try this delicious twist to your toast to maximize nutrients and support energy levels. Almonds supply heart-healthy fats and raspberries have antioxidant polyphenols, to nourish you and your baby.

Toast the slices of bread as preferred. Spread the almond butter over the toast and scatter the raspberries on top.

Sprinkle over the pumpkin seeds and drizzle a little more almond butter over the raspberries to serve.

Simple scrambled egg brunch

Serves 2
Prep 5 mins
Cook 15 mins

2 tomatoes, halved
1 garlic clove, crushed
3 tbsp olive oil
salt and freshly ground black
  pepper
4 eggs (choose red lion stamp
  for softly set eggs in
  pregnancy), lightly beaten
150g (5½oz) spinach
10g (¼oz) flat-leaf parsley,
  leaves and stems, roughly
  chopped
juice of ¼ lemon
160g (5¾oz) halloumi, sliced
2 slices of wholemeal bread
½ avocado, pitted and sliced

Flex it – *For a vegan version, swap the scrambled egg for scrambled tofu and remove the halloumi. Or, instead of the tofu, try Portobello mushrooms – grilled with a little olive oil – and add a generous spread of hummus to the bread.*

supplies iron • provides sustained energy

Never underestimate the humble scrambled egg – a pregnant woman's best friend. Brimming with nutrients, eggs provide iron, iodine, vitamin B12 (to help metabolize folate), and protein.

Preheat the oven to 180°C (400°F/Gas 6). Place the tomatoes on a baking tray, cut-side up. In a small bowl, mix the garlic with 1 tablespoon of the olive oil then pour evenly over the tomatoes. Season and bake for 10–15 minutes, until the tomatoes are softened.

Heat another tablespoon of the oil in a frying pan over a medium–low heat. Add the eggs, season, and stir frequently, until scrambled – the eggs should be softly set and forming curds. Remove from the heat.

While the eggs are cooking, heat the remaining olive oil in another frying pan over a medium heat. Add the spinach and stir for 2–3 minutes, until wilted. Mix through the parsley and lemon juice, season to taste, and remove from the heat.

While the eggs and spinach are cooking, grill the halloumi for 1–2 minutes each side, until golden brown. Toast the wholemeal bread as preferred.

Divide the tomatoes, scrambled egg, spinach, avocado, halloumi, and toast between 2 plates. Serve, finished with a crack of black pepper.

Simple scrambled egg brunch

Lunches and mains

Your main meals need to provide sufficient energy and nourishment to help you cope with the dramatic changes your body is undergoing, as well as support your baby's growth, aid your recovery post-birth, and fuel breastfeeding. At the same time, exhaustion and unwelcome pregnancy symptoms can make summoning the energy to cook a challenge.

The following chapter has a delicious selection of simple, appetizing, and flavoursome meals to nourish you and your baby. They also give you pleasure from the basic enjoyment of eating food, which can be social just as much as a necessity! Quick-to-assemble recipes are ideal for days when you feel fatigued, while a range of lighter bites and more substantial dishes cater both for smaller lunches and mains as well as for changes in appetite over the trimesters. Vegan, vegetarian, meat, and fish options are included with simple flex suggestions provided, offering ideas for removing or adding meat and dairy while still delivering key nutrients.

Choose from simple but colourful dishes such as filled wraps, pittas, or jacket potatoes; pizzas and pastas; or super-nutritious stir-fries, traybakes, and salads. For days when energy levels and appetite are healthy, crowd-pleasing dishes such as roast chicken, spaghetti Bolognese, and salmon nuggets are perfect. It's worth investing in good-quality airtight containers for batchcooking and freezing favourites, or to transport lighter meals when you're on the go. Each meal delivers a balanced range of nutrients, keeping you and your baby nourished and healthy throughout every trimester.

Pitta sandwich

provides sustained energy • provides antioxidants

When you feel sapped of energy, this classic and colourful warm pitta sandwich involves practically no cooking while delivering a delicious, balanced snack that will sate your appetite and supply a range of antioxidants.

Makes 1
Prep 5 mins
Cook 5 mins

1 pitta bread
2 tbsp green pesto
60g (2oz) mozzarella, sliced

100g (3½oz) roasted vegetables of choice (red onion, red pepper, and aubergine work well here; or make a day after the halloumi and okra traybake, see p.160, using any leftover veg)
1 tbsp olive oil

Slice a pocket into the pitta. Spread the pesto inside and fill with the mozzarella and roasted vegetables. (It can help to warm the pitta up slightly first to prevent it from breaking.)

Brush each side of the pitta with a little olive oil, then fry in a griddle pan over a medium heat for 1–2 minutes each side, pressing the pitta down with a spatula, until the cheese has melted and the pitta is golden. Serve warm.

Flex it – *Swap the mozzarella for cooked chicken breast if preferred; hummus also works as an alternative to pesto here.*

Chunky vegetable soup

Serves 4–6
Prep 15 mins
Cook 1 hour 15 mins

2 tbsp olive oil
1 large onion, finely diced
2 garlic cloves, crushed
15g (½oz) flat-leaf parsley,
   leaves and stems separated
   and roughly chopped
2 carrots, peeled and chopped
   into bite-sized chunks
1 swede, peeled and chopped
   into bite-sized chunks
2 potatoes, peeled and chopped
   into bite-sized chunks
2 parsnips, peeled and chopped
   into bite-sized chunks
2 tsp dried thyme
400g can cannellini beans,
   drained and rinsed
1–1.25 litres (1¾–2 pints)
   vegetable stock, plus extra
   if needed
salt and freshly ground
   black pepper
3 handfuls of spinach
crusty bread, to serve

provides antioxidants • promotes healthy digestion

Hearty, warming, and comforting, this soup is an all-in-one bowl of goodness. Abundant veggies together with cannellini beans provide fibre and antioxidants as well as supplying essential protein.

Heat the oil in a large lidded saucepan over a medium heat. Add the onion and fry for 8–10 minutes, or until soft and translucent. Add the garlic and the parsley stems and fry for a further minute or so to soften.

Add the carrots, swede, potatoes, parsnips, and thyme. Give all the vegetables a good stir, then cover with the lid and cook, stirring occasionally, for 10 minutes.

Pour in the cannellini beans and stock and season with a pinch of salt and pepper. The stock should just cover the vegetables; if not, add a little more. Bring to the boil, then reduce the heat to a simmer, cover the pan once more, and cook for 45–50 minutes, or until the vegetables are tender.

Remove the lid and add the spinach and parsley leaves. Cook for a further 5–10 minutes, until the spinach has wilted. Taste and adjust the seasoning. Serve piping hot with a side of crusty bread.

Rainbow sandwich

Makes 1
Prep 10 mins

2 slices of crusty bread
knob of butter
2 tbsp hummus
2 falafel, thinly sliced
mix of rainbow veggies
  – try cucumber, avocado,
  lettuce, yellow pepper,
  grated carrot, tomatoes,
  and cooked, cooled
  beetroot – all thinly
  sliced

provides antioxidants • provides sustained energy • promotes healthy digestion

A colourful array of vegetables ensures that this crunchy, quick to assemble sandwich is high in protective antioxidants, maximizing the nutritional benefits for you and your baby while also keeping your appetite satisfied.

Toast the bread as preferred, then butter one side of each slice of toast.

Layer the hummus, sliced falafel, and vegetables onto one slice of the toast. Top with the remaining slice of toast. Cut the sandwich in half and enjoy.

Any bean will do burrito

Serves 4
Prep 15 mins
Cook 20 mins

120g (4oz) white rice
2 tbsp olive oil
1 onion, finely diced
2 red or orange peppers,
    deseeded and sliced
2 garlic cloves, crushed
400g can mixed beans,
    drained and rinsed (or
    any preferred bean)
2 tsp smoked paprika
1 tsp cumin
pinch of chilli flakes
100ml (3½fl oz) passata
salt and freshly ground
    black pepper
4 large wholemeal tortilla
    wraps
sliced avocado and grated
    Cheddar, to serve

For the salsa
200g (7oz) tomatoes, finely
    diced
½ red onion, finely diced
15g (½oz) coriander,
    roughly chopped
juice of ½ a lime

supports heart health • promotes healthy digestion • provides sustained energy

Beans are a top source of fibre and plant-based protein, keeping you satisfied and maintaining energy levels. Pairing with avocado, peppers, and tomatoes adds heart-healthy fats and antioxidants.

Cook the rice according to the packet instructions then drain and set aside. In the meantime, heat the olive oil in a frying pan over a medium heat. Add the onion and peppers and fry for 8–10 minutes, or until softened. Add the garlic, beans, smoked paprika, cumin, and chilli flakes and fry for a further minute or so, until the spices release their aromas.

Add the passata to the pan, stir well, and allow to bubble. Season, lower the heat, and cook for 4–5 minutes, or until the beans are soft and the sauce has thickened.

To make the salsa, combine the tomatoes, red onion, coriander, and lime juice with a pinch of salt and pepper. Taste and adjust the seasoning if required.

To serve, arrange the rice and bean filling in a line down the middle of each wholemeal wrap and top with the salsa, avocado slices, and grated cheese. Wrap up the burrito and enjoy.

Flex it – *If you prefer, use chicken breast or chicken mince in place of the beans.*

Any bean will do burrito

Rainbow falafel bowl

Serves 4
Prep 30 mins
Cook 1 hour 30 mins

1 butternut squash, peeled and
   cut into bite-sized pieces
2 tbsp olive oil
salt and freshly ground black
   pepper
200g (7oz) quinoa
4 large handfuls of mixed
   salad leaves
8–12 falafel
200g (7oz) cherry tomatoes,
   halved
½ cucumber, diced
1 avocado, pitted and
   quartered
mixed seeds, to serve

For the beetroot hummus
1 large raw beetroot, about
   250g (9oz), topped and tailed
400g can chickpeas, drained
   and rinsed
1 garlic clove, peeled
1 heaped tbsp tahini
½ tsp cumin
juice of ½ lemon
2–3 tbsp extra virgin olive oil
roasted red and yellow peppers,
   courgettes, and cherry
   tomatoes, to serve

supplies folate • provides key micronutrients • aids fetal development

When nausea fades, say goodbye to bland fare and usher in the colour! This vibrant dish is full of antioxidant vitamins and minerals, as well as plant-based protein and folate from the falafel's chickpeas to support your baby's development.

Preheat the oven to 180°C (400°F/Gas 6). To make the hummus, wrap the beetroot in foil, place it on a baking tray, and bake for 50–55 minutes, or until easily pierced through with a knife. Allow to cool, then place in a food processor together with the remaining hummus ingredients and a pinch of seasoning. Blend until smooth and creamy, then adjust seasoning as required.

In the meantime, place the butternut squash on a baking tray. Drizzle with the oil, season, and gently toss the squash to coat it in the oil. Roast for 35–40 minutes, or until golden and the squash is soft all the way through. While the squash cooks, cook the quinoa according to the packet instructions.

To serve, divide the salad leaves between 4 bowls and top with the falafel, squash, quinoa, cherry tomatoes, cucumber, and avocado. Finish with a large spoonful of beetroot hummus and a sprinkle of seeds (any leftover hummus will keep in the fridge for up to 3 days). Serve with roasted vegetables on the side.

Rainbow falafel bowl

Easy pitta pizzas

Makes 4
Prep 5–10 mins
Cook 10–15 mins

4 wholemeal pittas
4 tsp tomato purée
80g (3oz) mozzarella, grated
8 cherry tomatoes, quartered
4 tbsp tinned sweetcorn,
  drained
½ orange pepper, deseeded
  and thinly sliced
10g (¼oz) basil, roughly
  chopped
freshly ground black pepper

Flex it – *Add ham for a meat-based
pizza. For a vegan version, swap the
mozzarella for a non-dairy version
and choose tempeh for bite.
Any leftover veggies can also
be swapped in here.*

**provides antioxidants • promotes healthy
digestion**

These quick-to-make, colourful pittas are a
nutritional win, supplying protein, fats, and
fibre-rich vegetables. Tomatoes and peppers
also add protective antioxidant carotenoids.

Preheat the oven to 180°C (400°F/Gas 6). Spread each
pitta with 1 teaspoon of the tomato purée and sprinkle
the mozzarella evenly over the pittas. Scatter over the
tomatoes, sweetcorn, and sliced pepper, then transfer
the pittas to a baking tray.

Bake for 10–15 minutes, or until the mozzarella is
melted and the pittas are crispy. Finish with a sprinkle
of basil and a crack of black pepper. Serve warm.

Asian-style greens stir-fry

Serves 4
Prep 25 mins
Cook 15 mins

4 tbsp dark soy sauce
1½ tbsp sesame oil
1½ tbsp honey or maple syrup
thumb-sized piece of ginger,
  grated
2 garlic cloves, crushed
½ tsp chilli flakes (optional)
400g (14oz) tempeh, cut into
  bite-sized chunks
4 tbsp rapeseed oil
160g (5¾oz) tenderstem
  broccoli, stems halved
160g (5¾oz) sugarsnap peas
200g (7oz) pak choi, chopped
3 large handfuls of kale
sesame seeds, to garnish
rice or noodles, to serve

Flex it – *Swap the tempeh for
4 chicken breasts, cut into strips,
or 4 salmon fillets. Marinate as
above, then cook in rapeseed oil.
For the salmon, remove the skin
and break the flesh into chunks.
Stir the cooked chicken or salmon
through the stir-fry before serving.*

**may help relieve constipation • may ease
nausea • promotes healthy digestion**

Refreshing and light, this is packed with fibre from
the abundant greens, to support digestion. Ginger
may help to lift nausea while the sweet and nutty
overtones of sesame stimulate the appetite.

Combine the soy sauce, sesame oil, honey or maple
syrup, ginger, garlic, and, if using, chilli flakes in a
bowl. Use 5 tablespoons of this sauce to marinate the
tempeh for 15 minutes. Set aside the remaining sauce.

To cook the tempeh, heat 2 tablespoons of the
rapeseed oil in a large frying pan over a high heat.
Add the tempeh and fry for 3–4 minutes each side,
or until golden and crispy. Set aside.

Heat the remaining rapeseed oil in a wok or large
frying pan over a high heat. Add the tenderstem
broccoli and fry, stirring frequently, for 3 minutes.
Add the sugarsnap peas and fry for a further 2 minutes,
then stir through the pak choi and kale until wilted.
Pour the remaining sauce over the vegetables and
stir until well combined and sizzling. Stir through the
cooked tempeh, sprinkle with the sesame seeds, and
serve with rice or noodles.

(photographed overleaf)

Asian-style greens stir-fry

Aubergine parmigiana

Serves 4
Prep 20 mins
Cook 50–60 mins

3 aubergines, topped, tailed,
and very thinly sliced
lengthways
3 tbsp olive oil
1 red onion, finely diced
2 garlic cloves, crushed
200ml (7fl oz) vegetable stock
700ml (1¼ pints) passata
1 tsp sugar
30g (1oz) basil, leaves and
stems, roughly chopped
salt and freshly ground
black pepper
300g (10oz) mozzarella,
drained and sliced

For the topping
50g (1¾oz) whole almonds
50g (1¾oz) breadcrumbs
30g (1oz) Parmesan, grated

Flex it – *For a vegan dish, use*
dairy-free alternatives to Parmesan
and mozzarella.

promotes brain health • supports heart health
• provides antioxidants

This popular dish is an antioxidant powerhouse
for you and your baby. Succulent aubergines supply
nasunin, which supports brain health, while cooked
tomatoes release heart-protecting lycopene.

Preheat the oven to 180°C (400°F/Gas 6). Arrange the
aubergine slices in a single layer over two baking trays.
Drizzle over 2 tablespoons of the oil, gently toss the
aubergines, and bake for 10 minutes, or until softened.

Heat the remaining oil in a pan over a medium heat. Fry
the onion for 8–10 minutes, until translucent and soft.
Add the garlic and fry for another minute. Add the stock,
passata, sugar, and most of the basil. Season, bring to
a simmer, then reduce the heat and cook for 15–20
minutes, until thickened. Adjust seasoning as needed.

In the meantime, make the topping. Blitz the almonds to
a crumb-like consistency in a processor, then combine
with the breadcrumbs, Parmesan, and a crack of pepper.
Arrange half the aubergine slices in a baking dish. Pour
over half the sauce, add half the mozzarella, then repeat
with the remaining aubergine, sauce, and mozzarella.
Sprinkle over the topping and bake for 25–30 minutes, or
until golden. Scatter over the remaining basil to serve.

Aubergine parmigiana

Salmon pesto pasta

provides sustained energy • promotes brain health • supports postnatal recovery

Transform pesto pasta with the simple addition of salmon and vitamin C-rich tomatoes. Salmon ensures this dish delivers on essential protein, providing energy and supporting postnatal recovery, and provides omega-3 to aid fetal brain development.

Serves 4
Prep 5 mins
Cook 15 mins

2 salmon fillets, about
  250g (9oz) each
1 tbsp lemon juice

200g (7oz) dried long pasta,
  such as pappardelle
190g jar basil pesto
50g (1¾oz) spinach, coarsely
  chopped
6 sun-dried tomatoes, chopped
grated Parmesan, to serve

Preheat the oven to 180°C (400°F/Gas 6). Wrap the salmon fillets in foil or baking paper to create a parcel. Before sealing, squeeze the lemon juice over the fillets. Bake for 12–15 minutes, depending on the thickness of the salmon fillets, until tender and the flesh flakes easily with a knife.

In the meantime, bring a pan of water to the boil and cook the pasta according to the packet instructions. Drain the pasta and transfer it to a large bowl, then stir through the basil pesto to coat the pasta.

While the pasta is still warm, add the spinach to the bowl and allow it to wilt slightly, stirring to combine with the pasta. Divide the pasta between 4 serving bowls. Flake over the baked salmon and sprinkle over the sun-dried tomatoes, and, if desired, a little Parmesan.

Salmon pesto pasta

Vegan carbonara

Serves 4
Prep 10 mins
Cook 20 mins

350g (12oz) dried spaghetti
2 tbsp olive oil
1 small onion, finely diced
100g (3½oz) mushrooms,
    sliced
1 courgette, thinly sliced
1 garlic clove, crushed
250ml (9fl oz) dairy-free
    single cream
3½ tbsp fortified nutritional
    yeast or vegan Parmesan
salt and freshly ground
    black pepper
chopped flat-leaf parsley,
    leaves and stems, to serve

supports bone health • provides sustained energy • provides key micronutrients

This creamy vegan version of the popular pasta dish includes B vitamins from mushrooms, and, if using fortified nutritional yeast, can help support energy production. Exposing mushrooms to sunlight enriches them with bone-supporting vitamin D.

Cook the spaghetti according to the packet instructions, then drain, reserving a little of the pasta water. In the meantime, heat a large frying pan over a medium heat and add the oil. Once hot, add the onion and fry for 8–10 minutes, until softened. Add the mushrooms, courgette, and garlic and continue to fry for a further 5 minutes, or until the vegetables are golden and cooked through.

Add the cream, nutritional yeast or Parmesan, and a pinch of salt and pepper. Stir well to combine, then cook for 2–3 minutes, or until the sauce has thickened slightly. Add the drained pasta and a dash of the pasta water to the sauce. Stir to combine, adding more of the pasta water if the sauce is too thick. Serve immediately, topped with parsley and a crack of black pepper.

Broccoli *and* cauliflower macaroni cheese

Serves 2
Prep 20 mins
Cook 30–40 mins

30g (1oz) butter
1 garlic clove, crushed
30g (1oz) plain flour
500ml (16fl oz)
   semi-skimmed milk or
   fortified plant-based
   alternative
1 tsp Dijon mustard
100g (3½oz) Cheddar,
   grated
50g (1¾oz) Parmesan,
   grated
salt and freshly ground
   black pepper
150g (5½oz) macaroni
100g (3½oz) broccoli,
   chopped into florets
100g (3½oz) cauliflower,
   chopped into florets
35g (1¼oz) panko
   breadcrumbs
green side salad, to serve

promotes healthy digestion • supplies folate

Cruciferous veg such as broccoli and cauliflower supply protective vitamins as well as fibre to keep digestion working well. Dark green broccoli also contains folate, supporting red blood cell production and your baby's developing nervous system.

Preheat the oven to 200°C (425°F/Gas 7). Melt the butter in a saucepan over a low–medium heat. Add the garlic and fry for a minute, until softened. Add the flour and whisk the butter into the flour for 2–3 minutes, to form a thick roux. Add the milk a little at a time, whisking vigorously with each addition for a smooth sauce. Stir through the mustard and bring to a simmer. Lower the heat and cook, stirring constantly, for 8–12 minutes, or until the sauce is thick enough to coat the back of a spoon. Remove from the heat, stir in the Cheddar and three-quarters of the Parmesan, and season to taste.

In the meantime, cook the pasta according to the packet instructions. Steam the broccoli and cauliflower florets for 5 minutes, or until tender when pierced with a fork. Add the pasta, broccoli, and cauliflower to the cheese sauce. Stir well and transfer to an ovenproof dish. Combine the breadcrumbs, remaining Parmesan, and a pinch of salt and pepper in a bowl. Sprinkle the mix over the macaroni cheese and bake for 20–25 minutes, or until golden and crispy. Serve with a green side salad.

Peach, mascarpone, *and* spinach salad

Serves 2
Prep 10 mins
Cook 20–22 mins

3 peaches, halved and pitted
1 tsp honey or maple syrup
1 tbsp olive oil
salt and freshly ground
   black pepper
4 handfuls of spinach
200g (7oz) mixed cherry
   tomatoes, halved
small handful of mint leaves,
   roughly chopped
100g (3½oz) mascarpone
15g (½oz) pine nuts, toasted
5 dried apricots, chopped,
   to serve
crusty wholemeal bread,
   to serve

For the dressing
juice of ½ lemon
1 tsp wholegrain mustard
2 tsp honey or maple syrup
4 tbsp extra virgin olive oil

Flex it – *For a vegan option, use dairy-free cream cheese in place of mascarpone and opt for the maple syrup over honey.*

promotes healthy digestion • supplies iron • provides key micronutrients

This light salad can be a godsend when your growing bump makes it feel hard to accommodate large meals. Apricot and spinach are a nutritionally dynamic pairing, delivering iron and fibre, as well as vitamin C, which supports immunity and aids iron absorption.

Preheat the oven to 180°C (400°F/Gas 6). Arrange the peach halves in an ovenproof dish cut-side up and drizzle over the honey or maple syrup and olive oil. Sprinkle over a pinch of salt and pepper, then roast for 20–22 minutes, or until the peaches can be pierced through easily with a knife.

To make the dressing, whisk all of the ingredients together, adding a pinch of salt and black pepper. Taste and adjust the seasoning if required.

Place the spinach, tomatoes, mint, and half of the dressing in a large bowl and toss together. Divide the salad between 2 bowls and top with the roasted peaches, crumbled mascarpone, the pine nuts, and apricots. Serve with a side of crusty wholemeal bread.

Peach, mascarpone, and spinach salad

Easy-peasy pasta bake

Serves 4
Prep 10 mins
Cook 45–55 mins

2 tbsp olive oil
1 red onion, finely diced
salt and freshly ground black
pepper
1 red pepper, deseeded and
finely diced
½ head of broccoli, chopped
into small florets
150g (5½oz) mushrooms, diced
2 garlic cloves, crushed
800ml (1½ pints) passata
1 tsp sugar
15g (½oz) basil, leaves and
stems, roughly chopped,
plus extra to serve
6 sausages (veggie or meat)
300g (10oz) pasta, such as
rigatoni
2 large handfuls of kale
100g (3½oz) Cheddar, grated

Flex it – *Swap Cheddar for a*
dairy-free alternative and opt for
vegan sausages to make this
a vegan dish.

provides sustained energy • supports a healthy gut • provides antioxidants

Packed with fibrous veg, vitamins and minerals, and fuelling carbs, this dish supports digestion and helps to keep hunger at bay for those times when pregnancy leaves you feeling ravenous.

Preheat the oven to 180°C (400°F/Gas 6). Heat the oil in a pan over a medium heat. Add the onion and a pinch of salt and fry for 4–5 minutes, or until the onion has softened. Add the red pepper, broccoli, and mushrooms and fry for a further 4–5 minutes. Add the garlic, stir, and fry for another minute, until the vegetables are softened.

Pour the passata into the pan, add the sugar and basil, then swirl about 3 tablespoons of water in the passata jar and add this to the pan. Season, then simmer for 15–20 minutes, or until the liquid is reduced. In the meantime, cook the sausages and cook the pasta according to the packet instructions until al dente. Once cooked, drain the pasta (saving a cupful of the water) and chop the sausages into bite-sized chunks. Set aside.

Add the kale to the pan and stir until wilted. Remove the pan from the heat and stir through the pasta (with the reserved liquid) and the sausages. Tip the mixture into a large baking dish and top with the cheese. Bake for 20–25 minutes, or until golden and bubbling. Serve sprinkled with extra basil.

Salmon nuggets

Serves 2
Prep 15 mins
Cook 35–45 mins

**2 large potatoes, chopped
   into chunky chips**
2 tbsp olive oil
**salt and freshly ground
   black pepper**
2 tbsp cornflour
1 tsp paprika
50g (1¾oz) breadcrumbs
**2 salmon fillets, skinned and
   cut into bite-sized chunks**
1 large egg, lightly beaten
4 tbsp mayonnaise
1 garlic clove, crushed
**leeks, courgette, peas, and
   mint (see p.166), to serve**

Flex it – *Replace the salmon
with 200g (7oz) of tofu for
vegetarian nuggets.*

**promotes brain health • provides sustained
energy • supports heart health**

Including a portion of oily fish each week in your
pregnancy diet provides essential omega-3s, key
for your baby's developing brain and your heart
health. These delicious fishy nuggets are a winner
with young and old alike – the perfect family meal!

Preheat the oven to 200°C (425°F/Gas 7). Combine the
potato chips, oil, and a pinch of seasoning on a baking
tray and mix well. Spread the chips out, then bake for
30–35 minutes, or until golden.

Place the cornflour, paprika, and a pinch of seasoning
in a bowl, combine, then tip onto a plate. Scatter the
breadcrumbs on a separate plate. Roll the salmon
chunks first in the cornflour mixture then in the beaten
egg before giving them a good coating of breadcrumbs.

Remove the chips from the oven and push them to the
sides of the baking tray. Place the nuggets in the centre
and return to the oven for 6–10 minutes, or until the
nuggets are cooked though (cut one in half to check).

In the meantime, mix the mayonnaise with the garlic and
a pinch of pepper until combined. Divide the chips and
nuggets between 2 plates and serve with the garlic mayo
and the Leeks, courgette, peas, and mint.

Beef *and* potato pasty

Makes 6
Prep 15 mins
Cook 1 hour–1 hour 20 mins

2 tbsp olive oil
1 onion, finely diced
2 garlic cloves, crushed
½ tbsp dried thyme
250g (9oz) minced beef
salt and freshly ground
  black pepper
400g (14oz) potato, peeled
  and finely diced
150g (5½oz) carrot, peeled
  and finely diced
1 tbsp plain flour, plus extra
  for dusting
2 tbsp tomato purée
500ml (16fl oz) beef stock
75g (2½oz) frozen peas,
  defrosted
1kg (2¼lb) shortcrust pastry
1 egg, beaten

Flex it – *For a vegetarian*
option, swap the beef mince
for Puy lentils and use a
vegetarian stock.

supplies iron • provides sustained energy

Lean red meat provides protein and iron, helping to energize you for the birth and beyond. Onions and garlic act as prebiotics, feeding healthy gut bacteria to promote overall health; and peas, potato, and carrot supply essential fibre.

Preheat the oven to 160°C (350°F/Gas 4) and line 2 baking trays with parchment paper. Heat the oil in a frying pan over a medium heat. Once hot, add the onion and fry for 8–10 minutes, or until soft and translucent. Add the garlic and thyme and fry for another minute or so to soften.

Add the mince, season, and fry, stirring constantly, for 8–10 minutes, or until browned all over. Add the potato, carrot, flour, and tomato purée and mix well. Pour in the stock and bring to the boil. Reduce to a simmer and cook for 25–30 minutes, stirring regularly, until the sauce is thick and reduced. Stir the peas through and cook for 1 minute. Season, then remove from the heat.

Roll the pastry out on a floured surface to about 3mm (⅛in) thickness. Using a side plate as a guide, cut out 6 circles. Add a few spoonfuls of beef filling to one side of each circle, brush egg wash over the edges, then fold each circle. Use a fork to indent and seal the rim. Place the pasties on the baking trays, brush with egg wash, and bake for 25–30 minutes, until golden. Enjoy warm.

Pea *and* feta couscous salad

Serves 4
Prep 15 mins
Cook 5 mins

250g (9oz) couscous
salt and freshly ground
  black pepper
150g (5½oz) frozen peas
200g (7oz) feta cheese
200g (7oz) cherry tomatoes,
  halved
handful of mint leaves,
  finely chopped, plus a
  few leaves to garnish
zest of 1 lemon

For the dressing
juice of 1 lemon
2 tsp honey or maple
  syrup
4 tbsp extra virgin olive oil

promotes healthy digestion • provides sustained energy • may help soothe anxiety

Fresh, light, and not too rich for a nauseous stomach, this salad delivers fibre, vitamin C, and protein, avoiding energy dips to help keep pregnancy anxiety at bay. Mint's aroma can also help to calm and the herb is a traditional remedy for digestive discomfort.

Combine the couscous and a pinch of salt in a large bowl. Pour over 250ml (9fl oz) of boiling water and stir. Cover with a plate and set aside for 10 minutes, then fluff up the grains with a fork.

In the meantime, bring a pan of lightly salted water to the boil. Add the frozen peas and cook for 2 minutes, then drain and set aside.

To make the dressing, whisk together the lemon juice, honey or maple syrup, olive oil, and a pinch of salt and pepper. Taste and adjust the seasoning as required.

Pour the dressing over the couscous and stir to combine. Crumble in the feta and stir it through, along with the peas, tomatoes, mint, and lemon zest. Serve the salad topped with a crack of black pepper and a few extra mint leaves to garnish.

Pea and feta couscous salad

Lemon *and* thyme roast chicken

Serves 4–6
Prep 10 mins
Cook 1 hour–1 hour 15 minutes
Rest 10 mins

½ **lemon**
**10g (¼oz) thyme, sprigs
    and leaves**
2kg (4½lb) whole chicken
2 tbsp olive oil
**salt and freshly ground
    black pepper**
3 garlic cloves, halved
1 onion, roughly chopped
1 carrot, roughly chopped

To serve
**either roasted or mashed
    potatoes and green veg
    of choice; or serve with
    the Potato wedges
    (p.174) and the Leeks,
    courgette, peas, and
    mint (p.166)**

may help improve sleep • supplies iron • supports immune system function

Chicken provides protein and a whole chicken has a range of nutrients. As well as vitamin B12, it has iron for energy and selenium to aid immune function. It also has tryptophan, a precursor to serotonin and melatonin, which may help promote restful sleep.

Preheat the oven to 190°C (425°F/Gas 7). Push the lemon and half of the thyme into the chicken's cavity. Rub the chicken with the olive oil, season, and push the garlic cloves under the skin where it gathers around the cavity.

Spread the onion and carrot over a large roasting tray. Sit the chicken on top and place the remaining thyme around it. Roast the chicken for 1 hour–1 hour 15 minutes, basting it halfway through. To check that the chicken is cooked through, pierce it with a knife and see if the juices run clear.

Cover the roasted chicken with foil or a clean tea towel and allow to rest for 10 minutes before carving and serving warm. Discard the roasted vegetables after carving the chicken. Alternatively, blitz them and add them to the roasting juices to make a gravy, or save them to use in the broth on page 213. Serve the chicken with potatoes and green vegetables.

Miso noodle broth

Serves 4
Prep 10 mins
Cook 20 mins

4 eggs (choose red lion stamp for soft-boiled eggs in pregnancy)
1.5 litres (2¾ pints) vegetable stock
5 tbsp miso paste
2 tbsp soy sauce
1 tbsp sugar
2 spring onions, finely sliced, plus extra to serve
thumb-sized piece of ginger, peeled and grated
1 garlic clove, crushed
½ red chilli, deseeded and sliced (optional)
200g (7oz) soba noodles
150g (5½oz) baby corn, halved
100g (3½oz) frozen edamame beans
200g (7oz) chestnut mushrooms, sliced
2 pak choi, quartered
sesame seeds, sliced spring onions, and sliced chilli, to serve

Flex it – *Replace the egg with crispy fried tofu, strips of steak, or fried cod loin.*

supports immune system function • may ease nausea • provides sustained energy

Nourishing throughout pregnancy, broths are perfect in the first trimester – comforting and filled with goodness for your growing baby. Ginger helps to relieve nausea while compounds in garlic and onions help support a healthy immune system.

Bring a saucepan of water to the boil and carefully add the eggs. Cook for 5 minutes, then drain and run under cold water to prevent them from cooking any further. Once cool enough to touch, peel the eggs and set them aside.

Combine the vegetable stock, miso paste, soy sauce, sugar, spring onions, ginger, garlic, and chilli (reserving a few slices for the garnish) in a large saucepan. Bring to the boil then reduce the heat and simmer for 5 minutes. In the meantime, cook the soba noodles according to the packet instructions. Drain and set aside.

Add the baby corn, edamame beans, and mushrooms to the broth. Bring back up to the boil, then lower the heat and simmer for another 5 minutes. Add the pak choi and simmer for another minute or so, until tender.

Arrange the noodles in the bottom of 4 bowls. Ladle the broth and veggies on top. Halve the soft-boiled eggs and add one to each bowl. Sprinkle with the sesame seeds, spring onions, and chilli slices, and serve immediately.

Miso noodle broth

Veggie chilli

Serves 4
Prep 10 mins
Cook 45 mins

2 tbsp olive oil
1 onion, finely diced
1 red pepper, deseeded
   and finely diced
2 garlic cloves, crushed
½ tsp chilli powder
1 tsp smoked paprika
1 tbsp paprika
1 tbsp cumin
1 tbsp dried oregano
salt and freshly ground
   black pepper
500ml (16fl oz) passata
2 tbsp tomato purée
2 x 400g cans mixed beans,
   drained and rinsed
200g can sweetcorn, drained
1 tbsp brown sugar
white or brown rice, chopped
   coriander, and guacamole,
   to serve

Flex it – *Remove the mixed
beans and replace them with
browned beef mince in step 2 for
a meat-based chilli if preferred.*

**supplies plant-based iron • promotes healthy
digestion • provides sustained energy**

This flavoursome, gently spiced chilli has
fibre-rich vegetables to support sluggish digestion
in pregnancy, while pulses provide essential iron
to energize you and support your baby.

Heat the oil in a large saucepan over a medium heat.
Once hot, add the onion and red pepper and fry, stirring
frequently, for 10–12 minutes, until soft. Stir in the garlic,
spices, oregano, and a pinch of seasoning. Cook for a
minute or so, until the spices release their aromas.

Add the passata, tomato purée, beans, sweetcorn,
and sugar. Add 3–4 tablespoons of water, stir well,
and bring to the boil. Reduce to a simmer and cook
for 15 minutes. Cover the pan with a lid and simmer for
a further 15 minutes, or until the sauce has thickened
and reduced. Taste and adjust the seasoning as
needed. Spoon the chilli over the rice, sprinkle with
the coriander, and serve with a side of guacamole.

Kedgeree

Serves 4
Prep 10 mins
Cook 25 mins

3 large eggs (use red lion stamp for soft-boiled eggs in pregnancy)
1 tbsp olive oil
1 onion, finely diced
250g (9oz) basmati rice
1 tbsp mild curry powder
½ tsp turmeric
500ml (16fl oz) vegetable stock
3 smoked and peppered mackerel fillets, skin removed
150g (5½oz) frozen peas, defrosted
15g (½oz) flat-leaf parsley, roughly chopped
lemon wedges, to serve

promotes brain health • provides key micronutrients

This comforting kedgeree is nutritionally dense. Eggs supply protein, iodine, and vitamin B12, while oily mackerel adds essential omega-3 fatty acids for brain health.

Bring a large saucepan of water to the boil and carefully lower in the eggs, making sure they are fully submerged. Boil for 6½ minutes, then drain and immediately plunge the eggs into cold water, until cool to the touch.

Heat the oil in a lidded pan over a medium heat. Once hot, add the onion and fry for 8–10 minutes, until soft and translucent. Add the rice, curry powder, and turmeric. Stir well and fry for another minute or so, until the spices release their aromas. Add the vegetable stock, bring to the boil, then lower the heat to a gentle simmer and cover with the lid. Cook for 10–12 minutes, or until the rice is tender.

In the meantime, peel and quarter the eggs and break the mackerel into chunky flakes. Once the rice is cooked, stir the mackerel, peas, and most of the parsley into the pan. Cook for 2–3 minutes, until the mackerel has warmed through and the peas are cooked. Serve the kedgeree rice in the pan topped with the soft-boiled eggs, the remaining parsley, and a squeeze of lemon.

Pearl barley *and* apricot tagine

Serves 4
Prep 20 mins
Cook 1 hour 15 mins

2 tbsp olive oil
1 onion, finely chopped
½ butternut squash, diced
1 courgette, diced
1 aubergine, diced
2 garlic cloves, crushed
thumb-sized piece of ginger,
  grated
500ml (16fl oz) vegetable stock
4 tbsp tomato purée
400g can tomatoes
400g can chickpeas, drained
  and rinsed
100g (3½oz) pearl barley
75g (2½oz) dried apricots,
  roughly chopped
salt and freshly ground black
  pepper
pomegranate seeds, flat-leaf
  parsley, and toasted flaked
  almonds, to serve

For the spice mix
2 tsp each turmeric and
  cumin, 1 tsp each ground
  coriander, paprika, and
  ground cinnamon, ½ tsp
  chilli powder

supports a healthy gut • promotes healthy digestion • supplies iron

This sweet and savoury winner uses an appetizing mix of spices, providing nutrient diversity. Chickpeas supply protein and resistant starch, which feeds healthy gut bacteria; apricots add iron and fibre; while ginger soothes nausea.

Heat the oil in a large saucepan over a medium heat. Add the onion and butternut squash and fry for 6–8 minutes, until slightly softened. Add the courgette, aubergine, garlic, and ginger and fry for a further 4–5 minutes. Add the spice mix and fry for another minute or so, until the spices release their aromas.

Add the vegetable stock to the pan, along with the tomato purée, tomatoes, chickpeas, pearl barley, and apricots. Season, stir well, and bring to the boil. Reduce the heat to low, cover with a lid, and simmer, stirring occasionally, for 45 minutes. Remove the lid and simmer for a further 15 minutes, or until the sauce is thick and the vegetables are tender. Taste and adjust the seasoning accordingly. Serve topped with the pomegranate seeds, parsley, and almonds.

Seafood paella

Serves 4
Prep 15 mins
Cook 45 mins

2 tbsp olive oil
1 red pepper, deseeded
   and sliced
4 garlic cloves, crushed
salt and freshly ground
   black pepper
100g (3½oz) green beans,
   halved
1 tbsp smoked paprika
1 tsp turmeric
2 tomatoes, grated
400g can butter beans,
   drained and rinsed
350g (12oz) paella rice
1 litre (1¾ pints) fish stock
250g (9oz) raw, shell-on
   tiger prawns
200g (7oz) live mussels,
   cleaned and debearded
chopped flat-leaf parsley
   and lemon wedges, to
   serve

supplies iron • provides sustained energy • supports heart health • aids fetal development

Warming and satisfying, this paella will help to keep energy levels up. Seafood is an excellent source of healthy fats as well as iron and zinc, all key for your baby's growth and development.

Heat the oil in a large frying or paella pan. Add the red pepper and fry for 6–8 minutes, until browned. Stir through the garlic, add salt, and cook for another minute or so, until softened.

Add the green beans, paprika, turmeric, tomato, and butter beans, and season. Stir, add the rice, and use a spatula to spread it evenly. Pour in the stock – if you can't fit it all, add the rest later, as below. Bring to a gentle simmer and cook for 10 minutes. Do not stir as the rice will be too starchy.

Reduce the heat to low and simmer for 8–10 minutes, adding any remaining stock, until all the liquid is absorbed. Add the prawns and mussels, pushing them down slightly into the rice. Cover, simmer for 6 minutes, then remove from the heat and rest for 5 minutes, covered, until the prawns and mussels are cooked through – the prawns will be fully opaque and the mussel shells open. Discard mussels that remain shut. Sprinkle over the parsley and serve with lemon wedges.

Seafood paella

Veggie sausage traybake

Serves 4
Prep 15 mins
Cook 45–50 mins

400g (14oz) new potatoes,
   halved
2 red peppers, deseeded and
   cut into strips
1 red onion, sliced
1 courgette, chopped
2 garlic cloves, crushed
1 tsp dried rosemary
2 tbsp olive oil
salt and freshly ground
   black pepper
8 veggie sausages
2 handfuls of cherry tomatoes
handful of flat-leaf parsley,
   roughly chopped, to serve

**provides sustained energy • may help relieve
constipation • provides antioxidants**

Easy to prepare, this traybake supplies plant-based
protein as well as fibre to help stimulate digestion.
An array of different-coloured veggies adds a
range of vitamins, including A, C, and K.

Preheat the oven to 180°C (400°F/Gas 6). Arrange
the potatoes, peppers, red onion, and courgette on
a baking tray. Add the garlic, rosemary, olive oil, and a
little seasoning, then use your hands to mix everything
together. Roast in the oven for 20 minutes.

Remove the dish from the oven and add the veggie
sausages and cherry tomatoes. Return to the oven
for 25–30 minutes, or until the sausages are cooked
through and the potatoes are going crispy on the
edges. Serve with a sprinkling of parsley.

Veggie sausage traybake

Butternut squash, spinach, *and* feta pie

Serves 4
Prep 15 mins
Cook 1 hour 15 mins to 1 hour 50 mins

1 large butternut squash,
   peeled, deseeded, and
   cut into bite-sized chunks
4 tbsp olive oil
salt and freshly ground
   black pepper
2 red onions, finely sliced
1 tbsp balsamic vinegar
1 tbsp brown sugar
200g (7oz) spinach
200g (7oz) feta, crumbled
2 tbsp pine nuts, toasted
4 sheets of filo pastry

**supports bone health • provides key
micronutrients • aids fetal development**

This comforting dish is full of goodness. Bright
squash contains carotenoids, which convert to
vitamin A in the body and support fetal development,
while feta provides protein.

Preheat the oven to 180°C (400°F/Gas 6). Place the squash
on a baking tray, add 2 tablespoons of the oil and a pinch
of salt and pepper, and toss to combine. Roast for 40–45
minutes, or until the squash is soft all the way through.

In the meantime, heat 1 tablespoon of the olive oil in a
frying pan over a low–medium heat. Add the onion and
a pinch of salt and fry, stirring regularly, for 8–10 minutes,
until the onion is very soft and starting to caramelize – add
a dash of water if the onion begins to catch. Add the
balsamic vinegar and brown sugar, stir well, and continue
to cook for 10–15 minutes, until the onion is dark-golden
and sticky. Remove from the heat.

Put the spinach in a colander and pour over a kettleful of
boiling water to wilt. Allow to cool slightly before squeezing
out any excess liquid. Stir the wilted spinach, roasted
squash, feta, and toasted pine nuts into the caramelized
onions. Finish with a crack of black pepper then transfer the
filling into a pie dish. Crumple up the filo pastry and arrange
it on top. Brush with the remaining olive oil, then bake for
15–20 minutes, or until golden and crisp. Serve warm.

Greek mezze bowl

Serves 4

Prep 15 mins

½ cucumber, diced

200g (7oz) cherry tomatoes, halved

½ small red onion, sliced

100g (3½oz) feta cheese, crumbled

2 large handfuls of mixed salad leaves

6 tbsp hummus

75g (2½oz) black olives

8 oatcakes, to serve

For the dressing

3 tbsp extra virgin olive oil

juice of ½ a lemon

1 tsp dried oregano

salt and freshly ground black pepper

Flex it – *To up your protein, add falafel or grilled chicken breast to this salad. For a vegan option, use a dairy-free alternative to feta.*

hydrates • provides sustained energy • supports heart health

This deliciously refreshing salad is a breeze to rustle up when pregnancy fatigue sets in. Olive oil provides heart-healthy fats, while hydrating cucumber and tomatoes help to keep you energized.

To make the dressing, place all the ingredients in a bowl and whisk together to combine. Taste and adjust the seasoning if required.

For the Greek salad, place the cucumber, cherry tomatoes, and onion in a large bowl, add 2 tablespoons of the dressing, and toss to combine. Sprinkle over the crumbled feta and gently stir this through the salad.

Divide the salad leaves between 4 bowls. Arrange the Greek salad, hummus, and black olives on top, and drizzle over the remaining dressing. Serve with a side of oatcakes.

(photographed overleaf)

Greek mezze bowl

Cauliflower *and* lentil dhal

Serves 4
Prep 10 mins
Cook 40 mins

1 cauliflower, chopped
  into florets
2 tbsp extra virgin
  olive oil
1 red onion, finely diced
2 garlic cloves, crushed
2 tbsp curry powder
125g (4½oz) dried red lentils
400g can tomatoes
600ml (1 pint) vegetable stock
1 tsp sugar
2 tsp white wine vinegar
salt and freshly ground
  black pepper
flat-leaf parsley, leaves and
  stems, roughly chopped,
  to serve

promotes healthy digestion • supplies iron • provides sustained energy

This warming, energizing dhal helps to maintain protein levels and provides fibre to ward off constipation. Lentils also supply iron, levels of which often run low later in pregnancy.

Preheat the oven to 180°C (400°F/Gas 6). Place the cauliflower on a baking tray, add 1 tablespoon of the oil, season, and gently toss together. Roast for 30–35 minutes, or until soft and beginning to brown.

Place a high-sided frying pan over a medium heat and add the remaining oil. Once hot, add the onion and cook for 6–8 minutes, until soft and translucent. Add the garlic, curry powder, and a dash of water. Stir well and fry for a minute or so, until the spices release their aroma.

Add the lentils, tomatoes, stock, and sugar to the pan. Stir well and bring to the boil. Lower the heat to a simmer and let the pan gently bubble for 20–25 minutes, stirring occasionally, until the lentils are soft.

Add the white wine vinegar and most of the cauliflower to the dhal, stir, and season to taste. Divide between 4 bowls, topping the dhal with the remaining pieces of cauliflower and sprinkling with a little parsley.

Prawn *and* tomato linguine

Serves 4
Prep 10 mins
Cook 15 mins

350g (12oz) dried linguine
2 tbsp olive oil
200g (7oz) cherry tomatoes, halved
3 garlic cloves, crushed
400g (14oz) peeled raw prawns
100ml (3½fl oz) vegetable stock
3 tbsp sundried tomato purée
salt and freshly ground black pepper
zest and juice of 1 lemon
2 handfuls of rocket

supports immune system function • provides key micronutrients

When fatigue leaves little energy for cooking, prawns are the perfect quick-cook, nutrient-dense ingredient, providing cell-building protein as well as essential selenium and immune-supporting zinc.

Cook the pasta in salted water according to the packet instructions. Drain once cooked, reserving a cup of the cooking water. In the meantime, heat a frying pan over a medium heat and add the olive oil. Once hot, add the tomatoes and fry for 2–3 minutes, until starting to soften. Add the garlic and fry for another minute or so, until lightly golden.

Add the prawns and stir well for 1 minute to coat them in the oil. Add the vegetable stock, sundried tomato purée, and a pinch of salt and pepper. Bring to a gentle simmer and cook for 2–3 minutes, or until the prawns are opaque and cooked all the way through (cut into one to check if you're unsure).

Stir the pasta, lemon zest, and rocket into the pan, adding a dash of the pasta cooking water to loosen the sauce if needed. Divide between 4 bowls and serve topped with a squeeze of lemon juice and a crack of black pepper.

Ratatouille

Serves 4–6
Prep 15 mins
Cook 50 mins

2 tbsp olive oil
1 onion, finely chopped
2 garlic cloves, crushed
1 aubergine, diced
2 courgettes, diced
1 red pepper, deseeded
 and diced
¹/₂ tsp dried oregano
1 tsp dried thyme
salt and freshly ground
 black pepper
400g can chopped
 tomatoes
15g (¹/₂oz) basil, roughly
 chopped
jacket potato, or couscous
 and raisins, flatbread,
 and yogurt, to serve

promotes healthy digestion • provides antioxidants

Enjoy a medley of colourful vegetables. This classic dish is bursting with antioxidants and is also a rich source of fibre, helping to avoid pregnancy-related digestive problems such as constipation.

Heat the olive oil in a large saucepan over a medium heat. Once hot, add the onion and fry for 8–10 minutes, until soft and translucent. Add the garlic and fry for another minute or so, until soft.

Turn the heat up slightly and add the aubergine, courgettes, red pepper, oregano, and thyme. Season, then fry for 12–15 minutes, stirring occasionally, until all the vegetables have softened slightly.

Add the chopped tomatoes and basil to the pan. Give everything a good stir, bring to the boil, then reduce the heat to a gentle simmer. Cook for 20–25 minutes, until the vegetables are tender and the sauce is thick. Season to taste and serve either with a jacket potato, or with couscous and raisins, flatbread, and yogurt. Alternatively, simply enjoy on its own or as a side dish.

Spinach *and* kale pesto pasta

Serves 4
Prep 10 mins
Cook 10 mins

300g (10oz) dried wholemeal
    pasta of preference
30g (1oz) basil, leaves
    and stems, plus extra
    to garnish
30g (1oz) spinach
30g (1oz) kale
1 garlic clove, crushed
20g (¾oz) pine nuts
20g (¾oz) Parmesan, grated
juice of ½ a lemon
5 tbsp extra virgin olive oil
salt and freshly ground
    black pepper
200g (7oz) cherry tomatoes
40g (1½oz) toasted almonds,
    roughly chopped
roasted red and yellow
    peppers, courgettes, and
    cherry tomatoes, to serve

Flex it – *Add chickpeas, chicken breast, or tuna if desired. For a vegan dish, replace the Parmesan with nutritional yeast.*

supplies folate and iron • supports heart health • provides key micronutrients

Add some simple extras to give your pasta and pesto a nutritional kick. Kale and spinach provide calcium, folate, and iron, all key in pregnancy, while nuts supply healthy fats and vitamins, to support you and your growing baby.

Cook the pasta in salted water according to the packet instructions. Drain and return to the pan, reserving a couple of tablespoons of the water for the sauce.

In the meantime, to make the pesto, place the basil, spinach, kale, garlic, pine nuts, Parmesan, lemon juice, olive oil, and a pinch of salt and black pepper in a food processor. Blitz until almost smooth (keeping a little texture), adding a dash of water for a thinner pesto if preferred. Taste and adjust the seasoning as required.

Add the pesto and cherry tomatoes to the pan with the pasta and the reserved cooking water and stir through to combine. Divide between 4 bowls and sprinkle over the toasted almonds and basil, and add a crack of black pepper. Serve with roasted vegetables on the side.

Sweet potato *and* chickpea curry

Serves 4
Prep 15 mins
Cook 40 mins

2 large sweet potatoes,
peeled and cut into cubes
3 tbsp rapeseed oil
salt and freshly ground
black pepper
1 onion, finely diced
2 garlic cloves, crushed
thumb-sized piece of
ginger, grated
2 tbsp mild curry powder
2 x 400g can chickpeas,
drained and rinsed
400ml can coconut milk
150ml (5fl oz) vegetable
stock
1 tsp sugar
juice of ½ lemon
50g (1¾oz) spinach
75g (2½oz) frozen peas,
defrosted
rice, sprigs of coriander,
and toasted cashew nuts,
to serve

supports a healthy gut • promotes healthy digestion • supplies iron

With fibrous sweet potatoes, chickpeas, and peas, this warming curry supports digestion and gut health. Chickpeas also supply iron, to help maintain energy levels in late pregnancy and postnatally.

Preheat the oven to 180°C (400°F/Gas 6). Put the sweet potatoes on a baking tray and add 2 tablespoons of the oil and a pinch of salt and pepper. Use your hands to mix everything together, then bake for 25 minutes, or until the potatoes are soft all the way through.

In the meantime, place a high-sided frying pan over a medium heat and add the remaining oil. Add the onion and fry for 8–10 minutes, until soft and translucent. Add the garlic, ginger, and curry powder, stir, and fry for a further minute or so, until the spices release their aromas.

Add the chickpeas, coconut milk, vegetable stock, and sugar. Season, stir well, and bring to the boil. Lower the heat to a simmer and cook, stirring occasionally, for 20–25 minutes, or until the sauce is thick and creamy.

Add the lemon juice, sweet potatoes, spinach, and peas and stir, adding a dash of water if the sauce is too thick. Simmer for another 2–3 minutes, until the peas are cooked. Taste and adjust seasoning as required. Serve with rice, a sprinkle of coriander, and the cashew nuts.

Sweet potato and chickpea curry

Salmon fishcakes

Serves 4
Prep 50 mins
Cook 10 mins
Chill 30 mins

**450g (1lb) potatoes,
   peeled and chopped**
1 tbsp butter
**3 spring onions, finely
   chopped**
**2 x 110g can salmon
   (or tuna if preferred)**
50g (1¾oz) Cheddar
2 eggs, beaten
4 tbsp plain flour
2 tsp dried chives
**salt and freshly ground
   black pepper**
50g (1¾oz) breadcrumbs
2 tbsp olive oil
**side salad and lemon
   wedges, or Leeks,
   courgettes, peas, and
   mint (p.166), to serve**

Flex it – *Replace the fish with
200g (7oz) of cooked chickpeas
for a vegetarian option.*

**promotes brain health • provides sustained
energy • aids fetal development**

Salmon provides cell-building protein and is a top
source of essential omega-3 fatty acids, supporting
your baby's brain development, while potatoes add
carbohydrates, for an all-in-one balanced meal.

Steam the potatoes for 10–15 minutes, or until tender.
Remove from the heat and leave to steam dry for
5 minutes in a colander. Heat a frying pan over a
medium heat and add the butter. Once melted, add the
spring onions and fry for 2–3 minutes, until softened.
Remove from the heat and tip in the potato. Mash the
potato into the onions, then add the salmon (or tuna if
using), Cheddar, 2 tablespoons of the egg, 1 tablespoon
of the flour, the chives, and season. Combine well and
shape into 4 fishcakes. Arrange on a plate, cover, and
chill for at least 30 minutes.

Scatter the breadcrumbs on a large plate and the
remaining flour on another. Dip each fishcake first into
the flour, then into the remaining beaten egg, before
giving them a good coating in the breadcrumbs.

Heat the oil in a frying pan over a medium heat. Fry the
fishcakes for 4–5 minutes on each side, or until golden
brown and heated through. Serve warm, with a side
salad and lemon wedges for a lighter meal, or with
the Leeks, courgettes, peas, and mint.

Spaghetti Bolognese

Serves 6
Prep 15 mins
Cook 1 hour 30 mins

2 tbsp olive oil
2 onions, finely diced
2 carrots, finely diced
2 celery sticks, finely diced
2 garlic cloves, crushed
salt and freshly ground
  black pepper
500g (1lb 2oz) beef mince
2 x 400g cans chopped
  tomatoes
200g (7oz) cherry tomatoes,
  halved
2 tbsp tomato purée
125ml (4¼fl oz) beef stock
2 tsp dried oregano
1 tsp dried rosemary
2 bay leaves
450g (1lb) spaghetti
Parmesan and chopped
  flat-leaf parsley, to serve

Flex it – *For a vegan version,
swap the beef mince for Puy
lentils, use vegetable stock
in place of beef stock, and a vegan
cheese in place of Parmesan.*

supports a healthy gut • supplies iron • promotes healthy digestion

This flavoursome Bolognese has fibrous veg for gut health while beef provides protein and iron. In addition, Parmesan contains *lactobacillus*, a gut-friendly bacteria that can help reduce gas, a common complaint in pregnancy.

Heat the olive oil in a large lidded saucepan over a medium heat. Add the onions, carrots, and celery and fry for 10–12 minutes, stirring regularly, until the vegetables are softened. Add the garlic, season, and fry for another minute or so.

Increase the heat and add the beef mince. Stir for 3–4 minutes, or until browned all over. Add the tinned tomatoes, cherry tomatoes, tomato purée, beef stock, oregano, rosemary, and bay leaves. Season, then stir well and bring to the boil.

Reduce the heat to a simmer and cover with a lid. Cook for 1 hour, then remove the lid and simmer for a further 15–20 minutes, until the sauce is rich and thick. Remove the bay leaves then taste and adjust the seasoning as required. Ten minutes before serving, cook the spaghetti in salted water according to the packet instructions.

Divide the spaghetti between 6 bowls, top with the sauce, and sprinkle over Parmesan and parsley to serve.

Spaghetti Bolognese

Veggie bean burgers

Serves 4
Prep 30 mins
Chill 20 mins
Cook 35–40 mins

400g (14oz) sweet potato,
   peeled and chopped
400g can black beans,
   drained and rinsed
50g (1¾oz) walnuts
2 tbsp tomato purée
2 spring onions, roughly
   chopped
1 tsp smoked paprika
salt and freshly ground
   black pepper
100g (3½oz) fresh
   breadcrumbs
2 tbsp rapeseed oil
4 burger buns
4 tbsp mayonnaise (or
   vegan alternative)
1 tomato, sliced
½ red onion, finely sliced
   into rounds
potato wedges (see p.174)
   and a green side salad,
   to serve

Flex it – *Use non-dairy
mayonnaise to convert this
into a vegan dish.*

promotes healthy digestion • aids brain health

These succulent, nutritious burgers supply plant protein from the beans; digestive-supporting fibre from the sweet potatoes; and omega-3s from walnuts, promoting brain, pregnancy, and postnatal health.

Preheat the oven to 180°C (400°F/Gas 6). Steam the sweet potato for 10–15 minutes, or until easily pierced with a fork. Remove from the heat and steam dry in a colander for 5 minutes. In the meantime, tip the black beans onto a baking tray and bake for 10 minutes to dry them out.

Combine the sweet potato, black beans, walnuts, tomato purée, spring onions, smoked paprika, and a good pinch of seasoning in a food processor on a high speed and blend into a paste. Add the breadcrumbs, then blitz again until the mixture is thick and keeps its shape when moulded. Divide into 4 balls, flatten into patties, and place in the fridge to chill for 20 minutes.

Heat the rapeseed oil in a large frying pan over a medium heat. Once hot, fry the bean burgers for 3–4 minutes on each side to crisp them up. Transfer to a baking tray and bake for 20–25 minutes, or until firm and cooked through.

Spread the burger buns with mayo and stack with the bean burger, sliced tomatoes and red onion. Serve with potato wedges and a green side salad.

Green pasta bake

Serves 6
Prep 15 mins
Cook 20–25 mins

**500g (1lb 2oz) pasta – penne
    works well in this recipe**
3 courgettes, grated
**250g (9oz) cherry tomatoes,
    halved**
250g (9oz) green pesto
**30g (1oz) basil, roughly
    chopped**
2 large handfuls of spinach
**200g (7oz) mozzarella,
    grated**
**salt and freshly ground
    black pepper**

Flex it – *If preferred, use
a vegan pesto and vegan
alternative to mozzarella.*

**promotes healthy digestion • supports immune
system function • supports a healthy gut**

Teaming spinach, courgettes, and tomatoes in this
delicious, filling bake provides fibre and vitamin
C, supporting immune system function and collagen
synthesis. It also provides a diverse nutrient
supply to help ensure a healthy gut microbiome.

Preheat the oven to 160°C (350°F/Gas 4). Cook the
pasta in salted water according to the packet
instructions until al dente. Drain, reserving
a cup of the cooking water, and set aside.

In the meantime, place the grated courgettes in a
colander over the sink and use your hands to squeeze
as much moisture from them as possible. Combine the
pasta, courgette, tomatoes, pesto, basil, spinach, and
a dash of the cooking water in a large bowl and stir
well to combine.

Pour the pasta mixture out into a large baking dish
and sprinkle over the mozzarella and a crack of black
pepper. Bake for 20–25 minutes, or until the cheese
is melted and bubbling.

Tuna, sweetcorn, *and* yogurt-filled baked potatoes

Serves 2
Prep 10 mins
Cook 1 hour 30 mins

2 large baking potatoes
1 tsp olive oil
salt and freshly ground
  black pepper
145g can tuna in spring
  water, drained
50g (1³/₄oz) tinned
  sweetcorn, drained
1 spring onion, finely
  sliced
45g (1¹/₂oz) Greek yogurt
1 tsp wholegrain mustard
30g (1oz) Cheddar, grated
green side salad, to serve

Flex it – *For a veggie option,*
try the favourite standby filling,
baked beans and cheese, or
fill with the Veggie chilli on
page 128.

provides sustained energy • promotes healthy digestion • supports bone health

Comforting, delicious, and satisfying, this simplest of meals is a nutrient powerhouse. Potatoes provide starchy carbs, fibre, and vitamin C, while tuna adds protein and bone-supporting calcium.

Preheat the oven to 160°C (350°F/Gas 4). Prick the baking potatoes several times with a fork, then use your hands to coat them in the olive oil and a pinch of salt and pepper. Place them on a baking tray and bake for 1 hour 20 minutes to 1 hour 30 minutes, or until crispy on the outside and fluffy in the middle.

In the meantime, make the filling. Combine the tuna, sweetcorn, spring onion, yogurt, and mustard in a bowl. Stir well to combine and season to taste. Chill until ready to serve.

Slice the cooked potatoes open and top with the tuna and yogurt mixture. Sprinkle with the Cheddar and finish with a crack of black pepper. Serve the potatoes with a green side salad.

Butternut squash pasta

Serves 4
Prep 15 mins
Cook 35 mins

4 tbsp olive oil
1 large onion, finely diced
2 garlic cloves, crushed
¼ tsp paprika
salt and freshly ground
   black pepper
1 butternut squash,
   peeled and diced
400g can cannellini beans,
   drained and rinsed
350ml (12fl oz) vegetable
   stock, plus a little extra
   if needed
30g (1oz) grated Parmesan,
   plus extra to serve
300g (10oz) dried fettuccine
15g (½oz) sage leaves
   and 30g (1oz) toasted pine
   nuts, to serve

Flex it – *Use a vegan alternative
to Parmesan if preferred.*

**provides sustained energy • supports immune
system function**

Staple pasta provides fuelling carbs for pregnancy.
Pairing with fibrous squash adds betacarotene
and vitamin C, helping to support immune function.

Heat 2 tablespoons of the oil in a large saucepan over a
medium heat and add the onion. Fry for 8–10 minutes,
or until soft and translucent. Add the garlic, paprika, and
a pinch of salt and pepper. Stir well and cook for another
minute or so. Add the squash, cannellini beans, and
stock. Bring to the boil, then reduce the heat to a
simmer and cook for 15–20 minutes, or until the squash
is tender and the stock has reduced by almost half.

Add the Parmesan and blend into a purée, adding a dash
more stock to thin the sauce if preferred. Taste and
adjust the seasoning. In the meantime, cook the pasta
according to the packet instructions. Drain, reserving
1–2 tablespoons of cooking water, and return to the pan.

Make crispy sage leaves by heating the remaining oil
in a frying pan over a medium–high heat. Add the sage
and fry for 30 seconds, or until crisp. Remove and drain
on a plate lined with kitchen paper.

Add just enough sauce to coat the pasta (freeze any
leftover) and the reserved water and stir to combine.
Divide between 4 bowls, topped with the Parmesan,
sage leaves, and pine nuts.

Butternut squash pasta

Sweet *and* sour chicken

Serves 2
Prep 10 mins
Cook 15 mins

1 tbsp cornflour
1 tbsp brown sugar
1 tbsp soy sauce
1½ tbsp rice vinegar
1 tbsp tomato ketchup
75g (2½oz) tinned
  pineapple, drained and
  juice reserved
salt and freshly ground
  black pepper
2 tbsp rapeseed oil
2 chicken breasts, chopped
  into bite-sized chunks
1 onion, thickly sliced
1 red pepper, deseeded and
  thickly diced
2 garlic cloves, crushed
thumb-sized piece of
  ginger, grated
white or brown rice, as
  preferred, and green veg
  of choice, to serve

Flex it – *Swap the chicken for
prawns if preferred, or for tofu
for a vegan dish.*

**provides sustained energy • supports bone
health • provides antioxidants**

If a sweet and sour craving hits, try this nutritious
dish before dialling in a sugar-laden takeaway.
White rice can be gentle on queasy tummies, while
pineapple provides vitamin C, key for collagen
synthesis to support your baby's developing bones.

Place the cornflour, brown sugar, soy sauce, rice
vinegar, tomato ketchup, 2 tablespoons of the reserved
pineapple juice, 100ml (3½fl oz) of water, and a pinch
of salt in a jug and whisk until smooth.

Heat 1 tablespoon of the oil in a wok or large frying
pan over a high heat. Once hot, add the chicken,
season, and cook for 4–5 minutes, stirring frequently,
until browned on the edges. Transfer to a plate and set
aside. Heat the remaining oil in the pan and add the
onion and red pepper. Stir-fry for 5 minutes, then add
the garlic and ginger and cook for a further minute or
so, until the vegetables are softened.

Return the chicken to the pan and add the pineapple
chunks, then pour in the sauce. Cook for 4–6 minutes,
or until the sauce thickens and the chicken is cooked
through – test the chicken by cutting the largest piece
and checking there is no pink flesh. Taste and adjust
seasoning as required. Serve with rice and green veg.

Halloumi *and* okra traybake

Serves 4
Prep 15 mins
Cook 35–40 mins

250g (9oz) giant couscous
2 green peppers, deseeded
**   and cut into strips**
1 red onion, sliced
100g (3½oz) okra, halved
2 garlic cloves, crushed
400g (14oz) halloumi cheese,
**   cut into cubes**
500ml (16fl oz) vegetable stock
2 tbsp olive oil
salt and freshly ground black
**   pepper**
75g (2½oz) pitted black olives
10g (¼oz) mint leaves, roughly
**   chopped**
10g (¼oz) flat-leaf parsley,
**   leaves and stems, roughly**
**   chopped**
juice of ½ lemon
green side salad, to serve

Flex it – *Swap the halloumi for chickpeas for a vegan dish. Or, for a meaty alternative, use mini chicken breast fillets or salmon fillets instead of the halloumi.*

supplies folate • supports bone health • provides sustained energy

Wholesome and healthy, this traybake will satisfy your tastebuds and help sustain your energy levels. Fibrous veg such as okra supply the B vitamin folate, while halloumi provides protein and calcium.

Preheat the oven to 180°C (400°F/Gas 6). Arrange the couscous, green pepper, onion, okra, garlic, and halloumi cheese on a large high-sided baking tray. Pour over the stock, drizzle with 1 tablespoon of the olive oil, and season. Stir to combine, then bake for 35–40 minutes, or until the couscous is tender and the halloumi golden.

Remove the tray from the oven and mix through the olives, mint, parsley, lemon juice, and the remaining olive oil. Serve warm with a green side salad.

Halloumi and okra traybake

Salmon, ginger, *and* cashew stir-fry

2 tbsp soy sauce
1 tsp toasted sesame oil
1 tbsp honey or maple
syrup
1 tsp rice vinegar
2 tsp cornflour
2 salmon fillets
3 tbsp rapeseed oil
thumb-sized piece of
ginger, finely chopped
2 garlic cloves, crushed
1 red pepper, deseeded
and sliced
100g (3½oz) broccoli,
cut into small florets
1 red onion, sliced
80g (3oz) baby corn, halved
lengthways
50g (1¾oz) cashew nuts
chilli flakes (optional) and
brown rice, to serve

Flex it – *If you can face bland food only, omit the salmon. For a vegan dish, marinate 225g (8oz) extra-firm tofu, cook for 3–4 minutes each side until golden and crispy, and use maple syrup.*

may ease nausea • promotes brain health
• provides antioxidants

Speedy, delicious, and nutritious, this is a go-to dish on those days when fatigue takes over but you're keen to keep your veggie quota up. Tummy-soothing ginger and brain-supporting omega-3s from the salmon make this a dish designed for pregnancy!

Make a marinade by combining the soy sauce, sesame oil, honey or maple syrup, rice vinegar, and cornflour in a bowl. Use 2 tablespoons of the sauce to marinate the salmon for 15 minutes.

In the meantime, heat 2 tablespoons of the rapeseed oil in a wok or large frying pan over a high heat. Add the ginger and garlic and fry for 30 seconds, then add the red pepper, broccoli, onion, and baby corn. Fry, stirring, for 5–7 minutes, or until the vegetables are tender.

Toast the cashew nuts in a dry frying pan for 1–2 minutes, until browned. Add the nuts and remaining sauce to the stir-fry and stir until combined and sizzling. In a separate pan, heat the remaining rapeseed oil over a medium–high heat. Fry the salmon, skin-side down, for 3 minutes. Once the skin is crispy, flip it and fry for a further 3 minutes, or until cooked through and the flesh flakes. Break into chunks and stir into the veggies. Sprinkle with chilli flakes, if using, and serve with rice.

Snacks and sides

This delicious selection of savoury and sweet recipes offers appetizing side dishes and tasty stand-alone bites.

Easy to rustle up on the spot or to make ahead for a ready-to-grab snack, these light bites are perfect for busy days and lazy evenings. They can also be ideal when uncomfortable pregnancy symptoms such as bloating and nausea make eating a complete meal a challenge, or, for example, when you need to reach for an energizing snack while feeding your baby. Flex options are included, with simple ideas for vegan diets.

Choose from delicious light bites such as sardines on toast, nutty trail mix, and savoury muffins and scones; enjoy tasty veggie sides; or try moreish snacks such as oat bars and stuffed dates.

Delicious and flavourful, these nutritious homemade snacks and sides support energy levels throughout the day as well as offer enjoyment – ultimately what you eat needs to be tasty and pleasurable, too!

Leeks, courgette, peas, *and* mint

hydrates • supports a healthy gut • provides key micronutrients

This juicy combo of vegetables with a hint of mint creates a tasty and refreshing side dish. Eating a range of veg not only delivers varied micronutrients, but also ensures a diverse gut microbiome. Leeks are also a prebiotic, feeding existing healthy gut bacteria.

Serves 4
Prep 5 mins
Cook 20 mins

2 tbsp olive oil
1 large leek, thinly sliced
1 courgette, sliced
salt and freshly ground
  black pepper
250g (9oz) frozen peas
15g (½oz) mint leaves, finely
  chopped, plus extra to garnish

Heat a large frying pan over a medium heat and add the olive oil. Once hot, add the leek and fry, stirring regularly, for 5 minutes. Add the courgette, season, and cook for a further 10–12 minutes, or until both the leek and courgette are soft.

In the meantime, bring a pan of lightly salted water to the boil. Add the peas and cook for 2 minutes, then drain and set aside.

Add the peas and mint to the frying pan. Stir well for a minute or so to combine all the vegetables, then season to taste, garnish with the mint leaves, and serve.

Leeks, courgette, peas, and mint

Sardines *on* toast

Serves 1
Prep 5 mins

**120g can sardines in extra
    virgin olive oil, drained**
juice of ¼ lemon
**1 tbsp flat-leaf parsley,
    leaves and stems, chopped**
**salt and freshly ground
    black pepper**
2 slices of wholemeal bread
knob of butter
handful of rocket
1 tomato, sliced

Flex it – *For a vegan toast option,
try hummus, sliced tomatoes, and
a sprinkle of toasted mixed seeds.*

**supports heart health • promotes brain health
• supports bone health**

An oily fish, the humble sardine is an excellent
source of omega-3s, helping to build cell membranes
and support brain and heart health. Eaten whole, the
tiny, edible bones supply bone-supporting calcium.

Mash the sardines with a fork in a small bowl. Stir
through the lemon juice and chopped parsley, then
season to taste.

Toast the bread as preferred. Spread the toast with a
little butter, then top with the rocket and sliced tomato.
Finish with the sardine mixture and a crack of black
pepper. Enjoy immediately.

Trail mix

Makes 15 portions
Prep 5 mins
Cook 10–15 mins

100g (3½oz) pecan nuts
100g (3½oz) almonds
100g (3½oz) cashews
75g (2½oz) pumpkin seeds
100g (3½oz) dried cranberries
125g (4½oz) dried apricots
75g (2½oz) dark chocolate chips

**supplies iron • provides sustained energy
• provides antioxidants**

Tasty and moreish, this energizing fruit and nut mix supplies fibre; iron and zinc; protein; healthy fats; and antioxidants. The perfect low-sugar snack, it avoids energy dips and spikes that can leave you feeling lethargic.

Preheat the oven to 180°C (400°F/Gas 6). Scatter the pecans, almonds, and cashews onto a baking tray and roast for 10–15 minutes, until browned. Allow the nuts to cool completely.

Place the roasted nuts in a large bowl with the pumpkin seeds, cranberries, apricots, and dark chocolate chips, and combine. Store in an airtight container for up to 2 weeks.

Avocado fingers *with* smoky lime mayo

Serves 4
Prep 15 mins
Cook 15–20 mins

2 tbsp olive oil
5 tbsp plain flour
salt and freshly ground
  black pepper
100g (3½oz) panko
  breadcrumbs
2 large avocados, halved,
  pitted, and each half
  cut into 4 slices
1 large egg, beaten
  (or use a flax-egg)

For the smoky lime mayo
75g (2½oz) mayonnaise
juice of ½ a lime, plus an
  extra squeeze, to serve
½ tsp smoked paprika

Flex it – *If you wish, replace the avocados with 400g (14oz) tofu, or use half and half. For a vegan version of this snack, use flaxseed egg instead of an egg and opt for vegan mayo.*

provides sustained energy • provides key micronutrients

Crunchy on the outside and soft in the centre, these irresistible bites make a nutritionally dense snack. With antioxidant vitamin E, fibre, and healthy fats, avocados are a good choice pre- and post-birth.

Preheat the oven to 180°C (400°F/Gas 6). Grease a baking tray with a drizzle of the olive oil. Tip the flour onto a plate and season with a pinch of salt and pepper. Scatter the breadcrumbs on another plate.

Roll the avocado slices first in the flour, then in the beaten egg, before giving them a good coating of the breadcrumbs.

Place the breaded slices onto the baking tray and drizzle the remaining olive oil evenly over the top of each one. Bake for 15–20 minutes, or until the breadcrumbs are golden and crispy.

In the meantime, make the smoky lime mayo. Combine the mayonnaise, lime juice, and paprika with a pinch of black pepper in a small bowl, then whisk until smooth. Serve the avocado fingers warm, with a squeeze of lime juice and dipped liberally into the smoky lime mayo.

Red pepper *and* coriander muffins

Makes 12
Prep 20 mins
Cook 25–30 mins

1 tbsp olive oil, plus extra
   for greasing
1 small red onion, finely
   diced
1 red pepper, deseeded and
   finely diced
salt and freshly ground
   black pepper
2 tsp smoked paprika
300g (10oz) self-raising flour
½ tsp baking powder
2 large eggs, lightly beaten
300ml (10fl oz)
   semi-skimmed milk or
   fortified plant-based
   alternative
150g (5½oz) Cheddar, grated
15g (½oz) coriander, leaves
   and stems, roughly
   chopped

provides antioxidants • promotes healthy digestion • provides sustained energy

Comforting and warming fresh out of the oven or perfect fuel when you're on the go, these savoury muffins supply key vitamins and are also full of fibre to help keep digestion moving in pregnancy.

Preheat the oven to 180°C (400°F/Gas 6). Lightly grease 12 holes of a muffin tin with olive oil. Heat a frying pan over a medium heat and add the olive oil. Once hot, add the onion and red pepper, season, and fry for 5–6 minutes, until the vegetables are softened. Stir through the paprika and fry for another minute or so, until it releases its aroma. Set aside to cool.

Sieve the flour and baking powder into a large bowl. Combine the eggs, milk, and a good pinch of salt and pepper in a jug, then slowly pour the mixture into the dry ingredients, stirring as you pour, until just combined.

Add the onion and pepper mixture, Cheddar, and coriander to the batter and stir through, then divide the mixture between the 12 muffin holes. Bake for 20–22 minutes, or until golden and a skewer inserted into the centre comes out clean. Allow to cool before serving. Store in an airtight container for up to 3 days or freeze for up to 1 month.

Red pepper and coriander muffins

Rosemary potato wedges

Serves 4–6
Prep 10 mins
Cook 35–45 mins

**4 large baking potatoes,
    chopped into wedges**
3 tbsp olive oil
2 tsp dried rosemary
**salt and freshly ground
    black pepper**

**provides key micronutrients • promotes healthy
digestion • supports immune system function**

With aromatic rosemary, these easy-to-make potato
wedges make a delicious side or a simple snack to
enjoy with a dip. The potato skin is especially rich
in fibre, while both the skin and fluffy centre
provide vitamin C and potassium.

Preheat the oven to 180°C (400°F/Gas 6). Bring a large
saucepan of salted water to the boil and add the potato
wedges. Return to the boil and cook for 2 minutes.
Drain and allow the wedges to steam dry in a colander
for 5 minutes.

Tip the wedges out onto a baking tray and drizzle with
the olive oil, rosemary, and a pinch of salt and pepper.
Give everything a good mix, then roast for 35–45
minutes, turning the wedges once halfway through,
until golden and crispy. Enjoy straight away.

Green falafel *with* tahini dip

Makes 10
Prep 15 mins
Cook 6–8 mins
Freeze 1 hour

400g can chickpeas,
   drained and rinsed
1 garlic clove, peeled
10g ('/₄oz) flat-leaf parsley,
   leaves and stalks
10g ('/₄oz) mint, leaves only
1 tsp cumin
1 tbsp tahini
1 tbsp lemon juice
salt and freshly ground
   black pepper
4 tbsp plain flour
4 tbsp rapeseed oil

For the tahini dip
60g (2oz) tahini
2 tbsp yogurt
2 tbsp lemon juice
¹/₂ tsp maple syrup
3 tbsp water

Flex it – *Use dairy-free yogurt*
for a vegan version.

supplies iron • promotes healthy digestion • supports bone health

Chickpeas, an excellent source of plant-based protein, provide essential iron and fibre, while the tahini-yogurt dip supplies B vitamins and calcium, supporting your baby's bone health.

Place the chickpeas, garlic, parsley, mint, cumin, tahini, lemon juice, and a pinch of salt and pepper in a food processor. Whizz into a chunky paste, stopping once or twice to scrape down the sides of the jug if needed.

Add the flour and pulse until the mixture forms a ball. Divide into 10 evenly sized smaller balls, then place on a lined tray and flatten slightly with the palm of your hand. Freeze for 1 hour, or until firm.

In the meantime, make the tahini dip. Mix all the dip ingredients together in a small bowl until smooth. Season well, then refrigerate until serving.

Remove the falafel from the freezer. Heat a large frying pan over a medium–high heat and add the rapeseed oil. Once hot, fry the falafel for 3–4 minutes each side, or until dark-golden and crispy. Serve the falafel warm, with the tahini dip on the side.

Bread "empanadas"

provides sustained energy • provides folate

Quick to make, these satisfying snacks help to keep you going between meals. Fortified bread provides folic acid, nutty and cheesy fillings supply protein, and fruit and veg provide key vitamins and minerals to support pregnancy.

Serves 4
Prep 5 mins
Cook 10–15 mins

4 slices of white bread
1 egg, lightly beaten

Filling options
peanut butter and banana
berries and chocolate spread
pesto and mozzarella

Preheat the oven to 160°C (350°F/Gas 4). Using a glass or a circular cutter, cut a circle out of the centre of each slice of bread. Flatten each circle out with a rolling pin.

Spread your chosen filling over half of the circle, leaving a 1cm (½in) gap around the edge. Fold the other half over the filling to create a semi-circle and use a fork to crimp the edges together, using some of the beaten egg to help seal the edges.

Brush the empanadas with the egg, then bake for 10–15 minutes, until golden and toasted. Serve warm.

Flex it – *To make these vegan, use plant-based milk instead of an egg wash to glaze the empanadas and keep the fillings vegan – use non-dairy cheese for the pesto filling, and a dairy-free chocolate spread to accompany the berries.*

Bread "empanadas"

Beetroot brownies

Makes 9
Prep 1 hour 10 minutes
Cook 30–35 mins

**2 beetroot (at least
300g/10oz combined),
scrubbed and topped
and tailed**
**250g (9oz) dark chocolate,
minimum 75 per cent
cocoa, roughly chopped**
200g (7oz) unsalted butter
3 large eggs
200g (7oz) caster sugar
50g (1¾oz) cocoa powder
150g (5½oz) plain flour
1 tsp baking powder
**50g (1¾oz) dark
chocolate chips**

supplies folate • provides antioxidants

Adding beetroot to these popular choccy bites makes
for a fabulously moist texture. Beetroot also supplies
folate, key for your baby's neural tube health, while
dark chocolate adds antioxidant flavonoids.

Preheat the oven to 160°C (350°F/Gas 4). Line a 18 x 18cm
(7 x 7in) brownie tin with parchment paper. Wrap the
beetroot individually in foil. Roast for 50–60 minutes,
or until they are easily pierced through with a knife.
Remove the foil and leave to stand for a minute or two.

Melt the chocolate and butter together in a bain-marie.
Remove from the heat and allow to cool slightly.

Measure out 250g (9oz) of the roasted beetroot and
purée in a food processor. Add the eggs and sugar
and blend to combine. Stir the beetroot mixture into
the melted chocolate, then sift in the cocoa powder,
flour, and baking powder. Fold until just combined,
then stir through the dark chocolate chips.

Pour the mixture into the prepared tin and bake in the
oven for 30–35 minutes, or until firm to the touch – do not
overcook the brownies; a skewer inserted in the centre
should come out slightly sticky. Leave to cool completely
in the tin, before removing and cutting into 9 squares.
Store in an airtight container for up to 3 days.

Cheese *and* chive scones

Makes 9
Prep 15 mins
Cook 12–15 mins

225g (8oz) self-raising
flour, plus extra for
dusting
1 tsp baking powder
salt and freshly ground
black pepper
55g (1³/₄oz) butter, chilled
and cut into cubes
90g (3¹/₄oz) Cheddar,
grated
35g (1¹/₄oz) Parmesan,
finely grated
1 tbsp fresh or dried
chives, whichever is
most convenient
90ml (3fl oz)
semi-skimmed milk or
fortified plant-based
alternative, plus
extra for glazing
butter or hummus
(optional), to serve

provides sustained energy • supports bone health

These moreish, tasty scones make the perfect
snack to fuel you between meals. A delicate
combination of herbs and cheese provides calcium
to support your growing baby's bones.

Preheat the oven to 190°C (425°F/Gas 7). Line a baking
tray with parchment paper. Sift the flour and baking
powder into a bowl. Add a pinch of salt and pepper
and stir though. Add the butter and use your fingertips
to combine with the flour to form a breadcrumb-like
texture. In a separate bowl, combine the Cheddar,
Parmesan, and chives. Add most of the cheese mixture
to the breadcrumb-like mixture, saving a little for the
topping, and stir through to combine.

Make a well in the centre of the mixture and pour in
the milk. Use your hands to bring the dough together,
being careful not to overwork it. If the dough is too dry,
add an extra dash of milk and mix again.

Lightly dust the worktop with flour and roll out the dough
to about 2cm (¾in) thick. Cut out 9 circles with a 5–7.5cm
(2–3in) cutter, transfer to the baking tray, glaze with milk,
and sprinkle over the remaining cheese and chive mix.
Bake in the oven for 12–15 minutes, or until golden and
a skewer inserted into the centre comes out clean. Enjoy
plain, buttered, or with hummus. Store in an airtight
container for up to 3 days or freeze for up to 1 month.

180

Cheese and chive scones

Kale crisps

Serves 2
Prep 5 mins
Cook 10–15 mins

200g (7oz) curly kale, woody
  stems removed and leaves
  cut into bite-sized pieces
2 tbsp olive oil
3 tbsp nutritional yeast or
  Parmesan
2 tsp garlic powder
large pinch of salt

provides key micronutrients • aids fetal development

When queasiness makes it hard to stick to your veggie quota, these moreish crisps are an excellent standby. If using nutritional yeast, look for a fortified version to provide vitamin B12, essential for your baby's development.

Preheat the oven to 160°C (350°F/Gas 4). Place the kale in a large bowl and add the olive oil, nutritional yeast or Parmesan, garlic powder, and salt. Massage everything together with your hands to combine.

Scatter the kale onto a baking tray and bake for 10–15 minutes, stirring once halfway through, until the edges are browned and crispy.

Apricot *and* courgette oat bars

Makes 8
Prep 10 mins
Cook 55–60 mins

2 large overripe bananas,
about 200g (7oz), mashed
3 tbsp honey or maple syrup
50g (1¾oz) butter or coconut
oil, melted
225g (8oz) rolled oats
50g (1¾oz) desiccated
coconut
150g (5½oz) dried apricots,
chopped
pinch of salt
100g (3½oz) courgette, grated

supplies iron • provides sustained energy

With less sugar than shop-bought bars, these oaty snacks release energy slowly, avoiding dips and spikes in blood sugar levels. The subtle addition of courgettes adds moisture as well as vitamins, while apricots supply both sweetness and essential iron.

Preheat the oven to 140°C (325°F/Gas 3) and line a 20 x 28cm (8 x 11in) brownie tin with parchment paper. Combine the bananas, honey or maple sryup, and butter or coconut oil in a large bowl. Add the oats, coconut, apricots, and salt.

Place the grated courgettes in a colander over the sink and use your hands to squeeze as much moisture from them as possible, then add them to the bowl. Stir to combine, forming a thick mixture.

Pour the mixture into the brownie tin, then use your hands to press it down and compact it into an even layer. Bake for 55–60 minutes, or until the edges are golden and the middle is firm. Allow to cool completely in the tin before removing and slicing into 8 bars.

(photographed overleaf)

Apricot and courgette oat bars

Stuffed dates

may support labour • supplies iron • provides antioxidants

There may be an ounce of truth in the folklore that dates lead to a more favourable labour as some studies suggest they may help to ripen the cervix – though with their high-sugar content, it's best to limit your intake to the odd treat. Team with pistachios and pomegranates to add antioxidants, and with apricots for iron.

Makes 12
Prep 5 mins

12 Medjool dates, pitted
6 tbsp almond butter
4 tsp pistachios, roughly chopped
4 tsp pomegranate seeds
4 dried apricots, roughly chopped

Fill each date with ½ tablespoon of the almond butter, then top 4 of the dates with pistachios, 4 of the dates with pomegranate seeds, and the remaining 4 with the dried apricots.

Refrigerate until ready to serve. The dates can be stored in an airtight container in the fridge for up to 3 days.

Cinnamon *and* honey popcorn

promotes healthy digestion • may satisfy cravings

Making your own popcorn is fun, healthier than eating
a shop-bought packet, and can satisfy sweet cravings.
Popcorn kernels also provide a little protein and fibre
to support your pregnancy diet.

Serves 4–6
Cook 10 mins

3 tbsp coconut oil
125g (4½oz) popcorn kernels
3 tbsp honey or maple syrup
1 tbsp ground cinnamon
pinch of salt

Melt the coconut oil in a large saucepan with a tight-fitting lid
over a medium heat. Add the popcorn kernels, stir to coat in the
oil, then put the lid on. Once you hear the popcorn begin to pop
continuously, shake the pan frequently until the popping stops.

Remove the pan from the heat and quickly add the honey or maple
syrup, cinnamon, and salt. Use a spatula to stir everything together,
then tip out into a serving bowl and enjoy while still warm.

Cinnamon and honey popcorn

Baked berry oats

Serves 1
Prep 5 mins
Cook 25–30 mins

1 large egg, lightly beaten
1 tbsp maple syrup (optional)
1 tsp vanilla extract
125ml (4¼fl oz) semi-skimmed
   milk or fortified plant-based
   alternative
45g (1½oz) porridge oats
½ tsp baking powder
handful of berries – blueberries
   and raspberries work
   well here
yogurt, almond butter, extra
   berries, and, if desired, a
   drizzle of melted white
   chocolate, to serve

Flex it – *To make this vegan, use a flax egg to replace the egg, opt for the fortified plant milk, and use vegan yogurt and chocolate.*

promotes healthy digestion • provides sustained energy

Enjoy this nourishing sweet snack any time of day. Fibrous oats release energy slowly, sustaining energy levels and helping you cope with fatigue. Berries add phytonutrient polyphenols, supporting brain health for you and your developing baby.

Preheat the oven to 180°C (400°F/Gas 6). Place the egg, maple syrup, if using, vanilla extract, and milk in a mixing bowl and stir to combine. Add the oats and baking powder and mix well, then gently stir through the berries.

Pour the mixture into a small ovenproof dish, then bake in the oven for 25–30 minutes, until golden and springy to the touch. Enjoy while warm, served with a spoonful of yogurt, almond butter, extra berries, and, if you wish, a drizzle of melted white chocolate.

Pineapple *and* spinach muffins

Makes 12
Prep 15 mins
Cook 20–25 mins

100g (3½oz) spinach
75ml (2½fl oz) buttermilk
1 tsp vanilla extract
75g (2½oz) butter, melted
110g (3¾oz) caster sugar
425g can pineapple chunks,
  drained
2 large eggs, lightly beaten
250g (9oz) self-raising flour
1 tsp baking powder

**supplies folate • provides antioxidants
• promotes healthy digestion**

These muffins work equally well as a snack or dessert. Including spinach supplies folate and antioxidant vitamin C, while pineapple adds natural sweetness and fibre.

Heat the oven to 160°C (350°F/Gas 4) and line a 12-hole muffin tin with paper cases. Place the spinach in a colander and pour a kettleful of just-boiled water over. When the spinach has wilted and is cool enough to touch, squeeze it between your hands to remove as much excess water as possible.

Place the wilted spinach, buttermilk, vanilla extract, butter, and caster sugar in a blender and blend until smooth. Add the pineapple chunks and pulse a few times to crush them into a chunky purée, allowing some texture to remain.

Transfer the mixture to a large bowl and whisk in the eggs until combined. Sift the self-raising flour and baking powder into the bowl and fold gently to combine, being careful not to over-mix. Divide the muffin batter between the 12 paper cases, then bake for 20–25 minutes, until risen and bouncy. Allow to cool completely before serving.

Date *and* walnut granola bars

Makes 12
Prep 15 mins
Cook 25–30 mins

225g (8oz) porridge oats
75g (2½oz) pumpkin seeds,
  or seeds of choice
100g (3½oz) walnuts, or
  other nut of choice,
  roughly chopped
100g (3½oz) unsalted butter
3 tbsp honey or maple syrup
100g (3½oz) soft, light-brown
  sugar
½ tbsp ground cinnamon
100g (3½oz) Medjool dates,
  pitted and roughly
  chopped

Flex it – *Use coconut oil in place of butter and opt for maple syrup instead of honey for vegan granola bars.*

promotes healthy digestion • provides sustained energy • promotes brain health

These satisfying snacks are also a nutritional treat. Oats release energy slowly, avoiding sugar dips between meals, and, together with dates, supply fibre to aid digestion. Walnuts provide omega-3s, supporting health and fetal brain development in pregnancy.

Preheat the oven to 160°C (350°F/Gas 4) and line a 20 x 30cm (8 x 12in) brownie tin with parchment paper. Place the porridge oats, pumpkin seeds, and walnuts on a baking tray, stirring them gently to distribute them evenly. Toast in the oven for 10 minutes, until lightly golden.

In the meantime, combine the butter, honey or maple syrup, and sugar in a saucepan over a low heat. Stir until melted, then remove from the heat and stir in the cinnamon, dates, and toasted oat mixture. Tip the mixture into the brownie tin, pressing it down lightly, then bake for 25–30 minutes, or until golden brown. Allow to cool completely in the tin before removing and cutting into 12 bars. Store in an airtight container for up to 1 week.

Oat *and* raisin cookies

Makes 10
Prep 30 mins
Cook 10–12 mins
Chill 15 mins

125g (4½oz) unsalted butter, softened
125g (4½oz) caster sugar
1 large egg, lightly beaten
½ tsp vanilla extract
pinch of salt
80g (3oz) wholemeal flour
½ tsp bicarbonate of soda
½ tsp ground cinnamon
150g (5½oz) porridge oats
125g (4½oz) raisins

provides sustained energy • promotes healthy digestion

Sweet and chewy, these tasty cookies can be a comfort in pregnancy. As well as satisfying sweet cravings, they provide fibre-rich oats, to support digestion and help sustain energy – an ideal snack in pregnancy or when breastfeeding.

Preheat the oven to 160°C (350°F/Gas 4) and line 2 large baking trays with parchment paper. Place the butter and caster sugar in a mixing bowl or processor and cream together until light and fluffy. Add the egg, vanilla extract, and salt and mix well to combine.

In a separate bowl, combine the flour, bicarbonate of soda, cinnamon, and porridge oats. Add the dry ingredients to the wet and mix well to form a dough. Stir most of the raisins into the dough (reserving some for the topping), then wrap in clingfilm and refrigerate for 15 minutes.

Use your hands to roll the chilled dough into 10 balls and arrange between the 2 baking trays, flattening the top of each cookie with your palm. Top with the reserved raisins, then bake for 10–12 minutes, or until golden at the edges but still soft on top. Remove from the oven and allow to cool before tucking in. Store for up to 3 days in an airtight container.

Date *and* nut energy balls

Makes 10
Prep 10 mins
Cook 10 mins
Chill 1 hour

75g (2½oz) nuts – whichever you prefer
50g (1¾oz) rolled oats
150g (5½oz) pitted Medjool dates
pinch of salt

Flavourings – choose 1 of the following
2 tbsp cocoa powder
zest of 1 orange
2 tbsp desiccated coconut
1 tsp vanilla extract
1 tsp mixed spice

energizes • promotes healthy digestion

Simple to make, these energy-dense and fibre-rich bites are a godsend when a below par appetite means you're struggling to meet your energy needs. Have a batch handy in the fridge or for when you're on the go.

Preheat the oven to 180°C (400°F/Gas 4). Spread the nuts and oats out on a baking tray. Bake for 8–10 minutes, or until lightly toasted.

Blend the dates, toasted nuts and oats, salt, and your chosen flavouring in a food processor until the mixture forms a thick ball – it may take a little time to come together, but continue blending.

Roll the mixture into 10 balls, place them in an airtight container, and chill for 1 hour before tucking in.
Store in the container in the fridge for up to 1 week.

Desserts and bakes

Sweet and satisfying, desserts and bakes tend to be an occasional, but looked-forward-to, part of our diets. They're often enjoyed with partners, friends, or family at weekends and on special occasions – or simply because it's been "one of those days".

This small selection of flavoursome and nutritious desserts and bakes uses naturally sweet fruits to intensify flavour, and adds crunchy nuts and seeds and creamy yogurt for texture.

Choose the easy-to-whip-up creamy pumpkin spice – a meal in its own right; enjoy colourful and refreshing yogurt bark; or bake a batch of sweet and delicious cinnamon swirls – with a fraction of the sugar found in shop-bought varieties – or a warming banana loaf.

Pumpkin spice dessert

provides antioxidants • supports bone health • promotes healthy digestion

Intensely tasty, this naturally sweet dessert – or light meal – is packed with nutrients. Cashews supply magnesium, for your baby's developing bones, and, together with the yogurt, some protein; while pumpkin provides fibre and antioxidants.

Serves 2
Prep 5 mins

225g (8oz) Greek yogurt
90g (3¼oz) canned pumpkin
   purée

¼ tsp mixed spice
2 tsp honey or maple syrup
4 tbsp granola
2 tbsp raisins
4 tsp cashews, roughly
   chopped

Place the yogurt, pumpkin purée, mixed spice, and honey or maple syrup in a bowl and combine until smooth and creamy.

Spoon a quarter of the mixture each into two glasses or mugs and top with a quarter of the granola, raisins, and cashews. Spoon the remaining pumpkin mixture on top before sprinkling over the rest of the granola, raisins, and cashews. Enjoy!

Flex it – *Use a dairy-free yogurt alternative and opt for the maple syrup for a vegan dessert.*

Pumpkin spice dessert

Fruity brownies

Makes 12
Prep 15 mins
Cook 25–30 mins

200g (7oz) dark chocolate,
   minimum 75 per cent
   cocoa, roughly chopped
170g (6oz) self-raising flour
3 tbsp cocoa powder
150g (5½oz) caster sugar
pinch of salt
5 tbsp rapeseed oil
250ml (9fl oz)
   semi-skimmed milk or
   fortified plant-based
   alternative
100g (3½oz) berries (such
   as a mix of raspberries,
   blueberries, and chopped
   strawberries)

supports immune system function • provides antioxidants • supports bone health

Chocolate and fruit are a winning combination and deliver a raft of antioxidants. Berries are especially high in vitamin C, supporting immune function as well as collagen production, for your baby's developing bones.

Preheat the oven to 160°C (350°F/Gas 4) and line a 20 x 28cm (8 x 11in) brownie tin with parchment paper. Melt 150g (5½oz) of the chocolate in a bain-marie or in a bowl in your microwave on the lowest setting. Set aside and allow to cool slightly.

Sift the flour and cocoa powder into a large bowl. Add the sugar and salt and stir through. Pour the oil, milk, and melted chocolate into the dry ingredients, then fold until just combined.

Stir the berries and remaining chocolate through the brownie batter. Pour into the prepared tin, smooth over the top, and bake for 25–30 minutes, or until springy to the touch. Cool for 15 minutes in the tin before transferring to a wire rack. Allow to cool fully before chopping into 12 squares. Store in an airtight container for up to 2 days.

Cinnamon swirls

Makes 12
Prep 15 mins
Cook 18–22 mins

150g (5½oz) plain flour,
  plus extra for dusting
1 tsp baking powder
pinch of salt
225g (8oz) Greek yogurt
50g (1¾oz) demerara sugar
1 tbsp ground sweet cinnamon
1 tbsp icing sugar, to serve

may satisfy cravings • aids fetal development

Light and delicious, these cinnamon bakes have less sugar and saturated fat than shop-bought equivalents, but bundles of flavour as well as protein. The perfect pregnancy pick-me-up!

Preheat the oven to 170°C (375°F/Gas 5) and line a baking tray with parchment paper. Combine the flour, baking powder, and salt in a mixing bowl. Add the yogurt and mix well to form a ball.

Transfer the dough to a clean worktop dusted with flour and knead the dough for 2–3 minutes, adding a little more flour if needed, until smooth. Use a floured rolling pin to roll the dough out into a rectangle, approximately 5mm (¼in) thick.

Place the demerara sugar and cinnamon in a small bowl and mix together. Sprinkle the sugar mixture evenly over the dough then roll it into a long sausage. Cut the dough into 12 spiralled slices and place them on a baking tray. Bake for 18–22 minutes, or until golden and cooked through. Serve warm, sprinkled with icing sugar.

Yogurt, berries, *and* chocolate bark

Serves 6–8
Prep 10 mins
Freeze 3 hours

500g (1lb 2oz) Greek yogurt
1 tsp vanilla extract
2–3 tbsp maple syrup, plus
    extra, to taste (optional)
30g (1oz) dark chocolate,
    minimum 75 per cent cocoa
50g (1¾oz) raspberries, whole
    or halved
50g (1¾oz) strawberries, sliced
10g (¼oz) pumpkin seeds
15g (½oz) granola

Flex it – *Use a non-dairy yogurt
and non-dairy chocolate for a vegan
dessert. Or to enhance gut-health,
try kefir instead of Greek yogurt.*

provides antioxidants • supports bone health • promotes healthy digestion

Nourish your pregnancy with this low-sugar alternative to ice cream. Yogurt provides protein and calcium for your baby's developing bones. Berries supply fibre and, together with dark chocolate, protective antioxidant polyphenols.

Line a baking tray with parchment paper. Combine the yogurt, vanilla extract, and, if using, the maple syrup in a large bowl. Taste and add a little more syrup if desired. Pour the yogurt mixture onto the baking tray and spread out with a spatula to form an even layer.

Melt the chocolate in a bain-marie or in a bowl in your microwave on the lowest setting. Drizzle the melted chocolate over the yogurt, top with the raspberries and strawberries, and sprinkle over the pumpkin seeds and granola. Freeze for at least 3 hours (ensuring the tray lays flat), or until the yogurt has frozen.

Remove from the freezer and break the yogurt bark into shards. Transfer into an airtight container, using the parchment paper to separate the layers, and store in the freezer until ready to serve. Freeze for up to one month in an airtight container.

(photographed overleaf)

Yogurt, berries, and chocolate bark

Vegan banana bread

Makes about 10 slices
Prep 15 mins
Cook 1 hour

4 large overripe bananas
85ml (2¾fl oz) rapeseed oil
100g (3½oz) soft, light-brown
  sugar
1 tsp vanilla extract
225g (8oz) plain flour
3 tsp baking powder
50g (1¾oz) demerara sugar
1 tbsp cinnamon

provides sustained energy • promotes healthy digestion

Comforting and moist, this banana loaf is a good source of fibre, which helps to lift sluggish digestion in pregnancy, and of fuel, which helps to stabilize energy levels across the day.

Preheat the oven to 160°C (350°F/Gas 4) and line a loaf tin with parchment paper. Use a fork to mash 3 of the bananas in a bowl. Add the oil, sugar, and vanilla extract and stir well. Sift in the flour and baking powder, then fold until just combined.

Pour half the batter into the loaf tin. Sprinkle over the demerara sugar and cinnamon, then top with the remaining batter. Use a knife to roughly swirl the cinnamon–sugar mixture through the batter before slicing the remaining banana in half lengthways and placing it on top. Bake for 50–60 minutes, or until a skewer inserted into the centre comes out clean.

Allow the loaf to cool in its tin for 10 minutes before transferring to a wire rack. Once completely cool, slice and serve. Or store, unsliced, in an airtight container for 2–3 days, or freeze uneaten slices for up to 1 month.

Vegan banana bread

Double chocolate cookies

Makes 10
Prep 15 mins
Cook 15–18 mins

155g (5½oz) soft, light-brown
   sugar
200g (7oz) plain flour
½ tsp bicarbonate of soda
25g (scant 1oz) cocoa powder
pinch of salt
125g (4½oz) dark chocolate,
   minimum 75 per cent cocoa,
   roughly chopped
70g (2½oz) almond butter
100g (3½oz) honey or maple
   syrup
65g (2¼oz) butter, melted, or
   coconut oil
1 tbsp semi-skimmed
   milk or fortified plant-based
   alternative

**provides antioxidants • supports immune
system function**

These divinely gooey chocolate cookies feed the
soul in pregnancy, while immune-supporting vitamin
E in almonds and antioxidants in dark chocolate
are a nutritional bonus for you and your baby.

Preheat the oven to 160°C (350°F/Gas 4). Line 2 baking
trays with parchment paper. Combine the sugar, flour,
bicarbonate of soda, cocoa powder, and salt in a
mixing bowl. Add most of the dark chocolate (saving
some for the topping) and stir it through.

In a separate bowl, combine the almond butter, honey
or maple syrup, melted butter or coconut oil, and milk.
Pour into the dry mixture and mix well to combine. The
dough should hold together when pressed between your
hands. If too dry, add a dash more milk and mix again.

Roll the dough into 10 equal balls. Space out the balls
between the baking trays and flatten each one slightly
with your palm. Divide the remaining chocolate
between the cookies and press into the top. Bake for
15–18 minutes, or until the edges of the cookies are
firm but the centres are still soft. Leave the cookies
to cool and firm up for 15 minutes on the tray before
tucking in. Store in an airtight container for up to 3 days.

Double chocolate cookies

Drinks

Drinking enough fluids is often overlooked, but hydration plays an important role in how we focus and function throughout life – especially when you're growing another human being. Staying hydrated during pregnancy, in labour, and when breastfeeding is crucial to ensure that your body is able to support the health and wellbeing of you and your baby.

Drinking water is the optimal way to keep your body hydrated. In early pregnancy, some women find that the taste of water is altered, so adding fruit, cucumber, and herbs is a great way to inject flavour. You can also try the following selection of caffeine-free hot and cold drinks for warming, flavoursome, and hydrating alternatives – something to suit everyone.

Here there are a selection of refreshing fruity or greens-based smoothies, ideal for getting some nourishment in, no matter how small the amount, when you can't face food. For hot drinks, intensely rich and warming chicken broth is packed with nutritional goodness, or try a soothing honey, lemon, and ginger infusion – one of my favourites. If you like a bit more variety and a spicy kick, sweet, delicately spiced vanilla chai milk is a delicious pregnancy pick-me-up to enjoy hot or cold.

Smoothie selection

Serves 1
Prep 5 mins

Almond and mango smoothie
1 overripe banana, frozen
150g (5½oz) mango
250ml (9fl oz) almond milk
20g (¾oz) porridge oats
1 tbsp almond butter
1 tsp vanilla extract
**25g (scant 1oz) vanilla
protein powder (optional)**

Blueberry smoothie
1 overripe banana, frozen
150g (5½oz) blueberries
**250ml (9fl oz) semi-skimmed
milk or fortified plant-based
alternative**
15g (½oz) porridge oats
1 tbsp pumpkin seeds
50g (1¾oz) Greek yogurt

Sneaky greens smoothie
handful of spinach
¼ avocado, flesh only
1 kiwi, topped and tailed, skin on
250ml (9fl oz) pineapple juice
**3cm (1½in) piece of fresh ginger,
roughly chopped**
1 tbsp hemp seeds
**25g (scant 1oz) vanilla
protein powder (optional)**

supports heart health • hydrates • energizes

Thirst-quenching and energizing, these nutrient-packed smoothies are ideal when you can't face food. Each smoothie provides heart-healthy fats, carbs, an abundance of vitamins and minerals, and some protein if you choose to add this.

Place all of the ingredients for your chosen smoothie in a blender. Add a handful of ice and blend until smooth.

For a slightly thinner consistency, add a dash more milk for the Almond and mango and the Blueberry smoothies and a dash more juice for the Sneaky greens smoothie, and blend again.

Chicken broth

Serves 4–6
Prep 10 mins
Cook 2 hours 30 mins

1 roast chicken carcass
2 litres (3½ pints)
   vegetable stock
1 garlic clove, crushed
1 leek, finely sliced
2 carrots, finely diced
1 tsp dried thyme
salt and freshly ground
   black pepper
handful of flat-leaf
   parsley, leaves and
   stems, roughly
   chopped, to serve

Flex it *– Remove the chicken*
and add more veggies as
desired for a vegetarian broth.

**supports immune system function • hydrates
• supports bone health**

This warming broth is the ideal way to use up a
roast chicken carcass. Used as a base for other
recipes, or enjoyed on its own as a drink or soup,
it provides collagen for healthy bones and is rich
in minerals, to support immune system function.

Set a large lidded saucepan over a medium heat.
Remove any remaining skin from the chicken carcass
and place it in the pan along with the vegetable stock.
(If you have leftover veggies from the chicken roasting
pan, add these, too.) Bring to the boil then reduce the
heat to a simmer and cover. Cook for 1 hour 30 minutes,
then remove from the heat and allow to cool completely.

Strain the broth through a fine sieve into another large
pan. Pick any remaining chicken from its carcass and
add to the broth, discarding any bones or gristle. Add
the garlic, leek, carrots, and thyme. Season, then bring
to the boil. Reduce to a simmer, cover with the lid, and
cook for 45 minutes–1 hour, or until the vegetables are
very soft. Taste and adjust the seasoning as required.
Strain once more. If you wish, blitz some of the veggies
and add to the liquid for a more soupy broth. Serve
warm, sprinkled with the parsley, either in mugs or in
4–6 bowls for a soup. Alternatively, allow to cool fully
before freezing for up to 1 month.

Honey, lemon, *and* ginger infusion

Serves 2
Prep 10 mins

2 tbsp honey
juice of ½ lemon, plus
2 slices to serve
1½ tsp freshly grated
ginger

supports immune system function • may ease nausea • hydrates

Refreshing and sweet, this traditional cold remedy is the perfect pregnancy infusion. Tummy-soothing ginger helps to quell pregnancy nausea, while vitamin C from the citrus supports immune system function, which is lowered in pregnancy.

Place the honey, lemon juice, and ginger in a large heatproof jug. Pour over 500ml (16fl oz) of freshly boiled water and stir well to dissolve the honey.

Allow to infuse for 5 minutes before pouring into mugs through a small sieve to catch the ginger. Finish off with a slice of lemon and enjoy while warm.

Vanilla chai milk

Serves 2
Prep 5 mins
Heat 5 mins

1–2 Medjool dates, pitted
½ tsp ground cinnamon
1 tsp vanilla extract
¼ tsp ground cardamom
¼ tsp ground ginger
pinch of ground cloves
pinch of ground black
   pepper
500ml (16fl oz)
   semi-skimmed milk or
   fortified plant-based
   alternative (oat milk
   works well here)

energizes • helps hydrate

This heavenly caffeine-free drink is a joy. The traditional spices and naturally sweet dates make this a delicious, fragrant beverage – the aroma being an integral part of our taste experience. Enjoy warm or chilled as preferred.

Place all the ingredients in a blender and blitz until smooth. Taste and add another date for sweetness if desired.

For a warm chai milk, pour the liquid into a saucepan and gently warm over a medium heat, being careful not to let the milk boil. If preferred cold, pour over a glass containing ice cubes and enjoy with a straw.

Index

Resources

National Childbirth Trust (NCT) www.nct.org.uk
Tommy's
www.tommys.org/pregnancy-information
Association of Breastfeeding Mothers abm.me.uk
La Leche League GB www.laleche.org.uk
The Breastfeeding Network
www.breastfeedingnetwork.org.uk/contact-us/
helplines (including in Bengali and Sylheti)
United Kingdom Association of Milk Banking
www.ukamb.org
Lactation Consultants of Great Britain www.lcgb.org
Pregnancy and anaemia www.tommys.org/
pregnancy-information/pregnancy-complications/
anaemia-and-pregnancy
The Miscarriage Association
www.miscarriageassociation.org.uk
The Birth Trauma Association
www.birthtraumaassociation.org.uk
Rhitrition+ (supplements to support pregnancy)
www.rhitritionplus.com

To access the studies and research supporting the
text in this book, visit: **www.dk.com/dhp-biblio**

A note on gender identities

DK recognizes all gender identities, and
acknowledges that the sex someone was
assigned at birth based on their sexual organs
may not align with their own gender identity.
People may self-identify as any gender or no
gender (including, but not limited to, that of
a cis or trans woman, of a cis or trans man,
or of a non-binary person).

As gender language, and its use in our
society, evolves, the scientific and medical
communities continue to reassess their own
phrasing. Most of the studies referred to in
this book use "women" to describe people
whose sex was assigned as female at birth,
and "men" to describe people whose sex was
assigned as male at birth.

Disclaimer

The information in this book has been compiled by way of general guidance in relation to
the specific subjects addressed. It is not a substitute and not to be relied on for medical,
healthcare, pharmaceutical, or other professional advice on specific circumstances and
in specific locations. Please consult your GP before starting, changing, or stopping any
medical treatment. So far as the author is aware, the information given is correct and up
to date as of April 2022. Practice, laws, and regulations all change, and the reader should
obtain up-to-date professional advice on any such issues. The author and publisher
disclaim, as far as the law allows, any liability arising directly or indirectly from the use,
or misuse, of the information contained in this book.

The recipes in this book have been created for the ingredients and techniques
indicated. The publisher and author are not responsible for specific health or allergy needs
that may require supervision. Nor is the publisher or author responsible for any adverse
reactions to the recipes in the book, whether followed as written or modified to suit
personal dietary needs or tastes.

About the author

Rhiannon Lambert is one of the UK's leading nutritionists, a *Sunday Times* best-selling author, and chart-topping podcast host. In 2016 she founded Rhitrition, a renowned Harley Street clinic, which specializes in weight management, sports nutrition, eating disorders, gut health, and ante- and postnatal nutrition. Its highly qualified, professional team of registered nutritionists, registered dietitians, and chartered psychologists work with individuals to transform their lives.

As an evidence-based practitioner, Rhiannon is committed to the benefits of a scientific approach to nutrition. She has worked as a consultant to many well-known food brands including Deliveroo, Wagamama, Alpro, Yeo Valley, and Little Freddie, refining their menus, product ranges, and cooking methodology. Rhiannon has also advised on nutrition and wellbeing at Six Senses, Four Seasons Hotels & Resorts, Microsoft, Samsung, and Coty. In 2017, Rhiannon published her first book, the best-selling *Re-Nourish: A Simple Way To Eat Well*, part handbook, part cookbook, in which she shares her food philosophy to lay the foundations for a happy, healthy relationship with eating. She followed this up with *Top Of Your Game: Eating For Mind & Body*, co-written with world snooker champion, Ronnie O'Sullivan. In 2020, Rhiannon wrote *The Science of Nutrition: Debunk the Diet Myths and Learn How to Eat Well for Health and Happiness*. A *Sunday Times* bestseller, with its accessible Q & A approach and informative graphics, this cuts through the noise of conflicting diet advice with clear answers backed up by the very latest research. Rhiannon also has her own food supplements company, Rhitrition+ @rhitrtionplus. A healthy, balanced diet should provide all the nutrients your body needs, but, sometimes, for all sorts of reasons, it falls short. Rhitrition+'s innovative approach uses Rhiannon's evidence-based, scientifically sound formulas to produce supplements for the vitamins and minerals lacking in many diets.

Rhiannon hosts the top-rated *Food for Thought* podcast, which gives listeners practical, evidence-based advice on how to achieve a healthier lifestyle. With more than six million downloads since 2018, it is firmly established as one of the UK's most popular health podcasts. Registered with the Association for Nutrition, Rhiannon obtained a first-class degree in Nutrition and Health, a Master's degree in Obesity, Risks, and Prevention, and diplomas in sports nutrition, and in ante- and postnatal nutrition. She is a Master Practitioner in Eating Disorders, accredited by The British Psychological Society, and a Level 3 Personal Trainer. Follow Rhiannon on Instagram, Twitter, Facebook, TikTok and YouTube at @Rhitrition and visit Rhitrition.com.

Author's acknowledgments

Writing this book, which I wish I had been able to read before I first gave birth, has been harder than I thought, but more rewarding than I could have ever imagined. Writing about something so personal in life is a surreal process, and so I am indebted to everyone at DK for letting me shape this book and for inviting me to be a part of your amazing community.

I am still learning, every single day, so it is only with the help and support of a number of key contributors that I can share advice so confidently. Marie Louise, Dr Anjali Amin, Stacey Zimmels, Anna Mathur, and Charlie Launder – you all deserve the biggest thank you for helping to bring this book to life.

In what has been the most difficult few years, embracing motherhood while reaching for a work–life balance – challenged further by writing in lockdown – I am so lucky to have so many wonderful people by my side, but without the encouragement of my Rhitrition team – in particular Bea Moore and Eleanor Morris – and husband Billy, I would not have been afforded the time required to make this book a reality.

Publisher's acknowledgments

DK would like to thank: Rhiannon Lambert for her guidance and expertise. Also, Claire Wedderburn-Maxwell for proofreading, and Hilary Bird for indexing.

Contributors

Dr Anjali Amin @thekitchendoctorandmum; hormones in pregnancy
Marie Louise @themodernmidwife; eating in labour
Anna Mathur @annamathur; postnatal depression (PND)
Stacey Zimmels @feedeatspeak; lactation consultant
Charlie Launder @bumpsandburpees; exercising in pregnancy

Penguin Random House

Senior Project Editor	Claire Cross
Senior Project Designers	Emma Forge and Tom Forge
Senior Designer	Barbara Zuniga
Project Editor	Izzy Holton
Jacket Designer	Amy Cox
Jacket Coordinator	Jasmin Lennie
Senior Production Editor	Tony Phipps
Senior Producer	Luca Bazzoli
DTP and Design Coordinator	Heather Blagden
Editorial Manager	Ruth O'Rourke
Design Manager	Marianne Markham
Art Director	Maxine Pedliham
Publishing Director	Katie Cowan
Photographer	Luke Albert
Food and Prop Stylist	Libby Silbermann

First published in Great Britain in 2022 by
Dorling Kindersley Limited
DK, One Embassy Gardens, 8 Viaduct Gardens,
London, SW11 7BW

The authorised representative in the EEA is
Dorling Kindersley Verlag GmbH.
Arnulfstr. 124, 80636 Munich, Germany

A CIP catalogue record for this book
is available from the British Library.
ISBN: 978-0-2415-3056-6

Printed and bound in China

For the curious
www.dk.com

This book was made with Forest Stewardship Council™
certified paper – one small step in DK's
commitment to a sustainable future.
For more information go to www.dk.com/our-green-pledge